Documenting Maritime Heritage at Risk

Documenting Maritime Heritage at Risk addresses the risks posed to coastal piers and quays due to climate change, the urgent need for documentation and attendant questions regarding long-term conservation, and the role communities could have in this endeavour.

Case studies from communities, researchers, and national agencies offer insights into the documentation and analysis of coastal heritage, guidance on survey methodologies, and the potential of digital tools. Communities living along the coast, who are deeply attached to their heritage, are facing these threats very directly – and often with a sense of having little agency in the discussions or decisions being taken. Yet, as the book demonstrates, they could have a central role to play as first-hand observers of the impact of climate change on their heritage. The collection offers an overview of the invaluable role of different participants, working collectively in the documentation and management of endangered maritime heritage.

Documenting Maritime Heritage at Risk provides a vital resource for researchers and students engaged in the study of maritime heritage. It will also be of great interest to practitioners, such as local heritage or conservation officers and marine engineers who bear the primary responsibility for recording and maintaining maritime heritage.

Elizabeth Shotton is Associate Professor at the University College Dublin Ireland.

Oriel Prizeman is Professor at Cardiff University (Wales), UK.

Documenting Maritime Heritage at Risk

Digital Tools, Communities, and Institutions

Edited by Elizabeth Shotton and Oriel Prizeman

LONDON AND NEW YORK

First published 2024
by Routledge
4 Park Square, Milton Park, Abingdon, Oxon OX14 4RN

and by Routledge
605 Third Avenue, New York, NY 10158

Routledge is an imprint of the Taylor & Francis Group, an informa business

© 2024 selection and editorial matter, Elizabeth Shotton and Oriel Prizeman; individual chapters, the contributors

The right of Elizabeth Shotton and Oriel Prizeman to be identified as the authors of the editorial material, and of the authors for their individual chapters, has been asserted in accordance with sections 77 and 78 of the Copyright, Designs and Patents Act 1988.

The Open Access version of this book, available at www.taylorfrancis.com, has been made available under a Creative Commons Attribution-Non Commercial-No Derivatives (CC-BY-NC-ND) 4.0 International license.

Trademark notice: Product or corporate names may be trademarks or registered trademarks, and are used only for identification and explanation without intent to infringe.

British Library Cataloguing-in-Publication Data
A catalogue record for this book is available from the British Library

ISBN: 978-1-032-47208-9 (hbk)
ISBN: 978-1-032-47210-2 (pbk)
ISBN: 978-1-003-38509-7 (ebk)

DOI: 10.4324/9781003385097

Typeset in Times New Roman
by Apex CoVantage, LLC

Contents

Contributors		*vii*
Foreword		*ix*
Mario Santana Quintero		
Acknowledgements		*xi*

1	**Coastal Heritage, Communities & Climate Change**	1
	ELIZABETH SHOTTON	

SECTION 1
Inventories, Classifications & Management 13

2	**Inventories of Maritime Heritage**	15
	ELIZABETH SHOTTON	

3	**Small-Scale Harbours: A Framework Approach to Site Assessment and Classification**	28
	HILARY WYATT	

4	**The Role of National and Regional Bodies: The Historic Harbours of Wales**	42
	JULIAN WHITEWRIGHT	

SECTION 2
The Role of Communities 53

5	**Recording Our Historic Harbours**	55
	BILL HASTINGS	

| 6 | The Role and Purpose of Digital Documentation for Marginal Heritage | 67 |

ORIEL PRIZEMAN

| 7 | Ballydehob Quay and Its Small Satellite Quays | 78 |

CORMAC LEVIS

Epilogue 91

| 8 | The Future of Harbour Heritage | 93 |

LINDE EGBERTS AND ELIZABETH SHOTTON

Resources for Communities   *103*
Index   *105*

Contributors

Dr Linde Egberts, Knowledge Strategy Coordinator, Cultural Heritage Agency of the Netherlands, Ministry of Education, Culture and Science (the Netherlands). Dr Egberts was trained as a human geographer and cultural historian at Utrecht University and Vrije Universiteit Amsterdam and works in the interdisciplinary field of Critical Heritage Studies. Dr Egberts has recently taken up a position to lead the new research strategy of the Cultural Heritage Agency of the Netherlands.

Bill Hastings, ARC Architectural Consultants (Ireland). Bill Hastings is a conservation architect practicing in architecture, conservation, and measured survey, He has taught conservation, surveying and the photographic recording of historic structures at University College Dublin since 1976.

Cormac Levis, Local Historian, West Cork (Ireland). Cormac Levis is a local maritime historian who has researched and written extensively on the traditional workboats and trading vessels of Roaringwater Bay, West Cork.

Prof Oriel Prizeman, Professor, Cardiff University (Wales). Prof Prizeman's research focuses on building environmental histories and digital tools for conservation including HBIM. She started the MSc in Sustainable Building Conservation and leads the Centre for Sustainable Building Conservation at the Welsh School of Architecture (WSA).

Prof Mario Santana Quintero, Professor, Carleton University (Canada). Prof Santana-Quintero is a member of the Carleton Immersive Media Studio Lab (CIMS), guest professor at the KU Leuven, Secretary General of the International Council of Monuments and Sites (ICOMOS) and Honorary President of the ICOMOS Scientific Committee on Heritage Documentation (CIPA). He collaborates extensively in international projects in the field of heritage documentation with the Getty Conservation Institute and UNESCO among others.

Dr Elizabeth Shotton, Associate Professor, University College Dublin (Ireland). Dr Shotton is an architect who teaches construction technology and design at the UCD School of Architecture, Planning, and Environmental Policy. She leads the Minor Harbours of Ireland (MHI) study on small harbours along the coast of Ireland from the seventeenth century to the present.

Dr Julian Whitewright, Senior Investigator (Maritime), Royal Commission on the Ancient and Historical Monuments of Wales. Dr Whitewright, a maritime archaeologist who has practiced internationally, has recently taken a post as Senior Investigator (Maritime) at the RCAHMW. His current appointment addresses all aspects of maritime archaeology, including harbours.

Hilary Wyatt, Cardiff University (Wales). Hilary Wyatt, PGDip Surv (Reading), MSc Sustainable Building Conservation (Cardiff) is currently an EPSRC-funded PhD candidate at the Welsh School of Architecture. Her research into inter-tidal structures and harbour settings is interdisciplinary, informed both by her professional practice and former experience of coastal navigation.

Foreword

Volk *et al.* argue that the "phenomenon of global sea level rise is transforming landscapes, exacerbating risks to human settlements and economies, and forcing societies not only to seek ways to mitigate changes but also to adapt to the inevitable" (Volk, Frank, and Nettles 2015, 227), which is very relevant to heritage places located in coastal areas. *Documenting Maritime Cultural Heritage* draws attention toward vulnerable heritage places subjected to the well-studied phenomena of sea level rises but not studied because of a lack of worldwide appreciation and recognition from conventional heritage protection frameworks.

This book, structured in two sections and eight chapters with articles and a panel discussion, provides practical and valuable contributions to the body of knowledge in identifying and documenting those sites using state-of-the-art digital technologies based on experience gathered by working in marginalised maritime cultural heritage.

As a heritage recording professional, honorary president of the International Council of Monuments and Sites (ICOMOS) Scientific Committee on Heritage Documentation (CIPA), and ICOMOS Secretary General, I have experienced first the increasing need to use comprehensive inventory policies that address a broader scope (and views) to understand the built environment in an ever-changing heritage field. The results of academic manuscripts by important scholars, scientific conferences and international organisations around the vulnerability of important places, such as UNESCO World Heritage Sites, are vast and relevant. However, the approaches are often unachievable to sites lacking interest, financial resources and recognition; nearly nothing has been published about marginal heritage, which is equally threatened and neglected, but essential to local communities.

Furthermore, Kansa exposes that 'we need more inclusive thinking about data, especially in how data reflect the interests of our stakeholders' (Kansa 2022, 8); this book provides practices for inventories and the use of digital technologies and emphasizes the crucial involvement of communities to provide the required invaluable local knowledge and to monitor the state of conservation of these vulnerable coastal sites.

For ICOMOS and the heritage conservation experts, *Documenting Maritime Cultural Heritage* could offer tools to increase the capacity of regional and national bodies responsible for such inventories and local communities that assist in the documentation processes to create posterity records for those sites that inevitably will disappear and opportunities to protect those that can be saved. I highly recommend that the authorities and practitioners adopt this book to address these critical vulnerable places, eventually producing policies, strategies and other protocols to implement in other world settings.

This book can also be used as a template to assess other marginalised heritage places offering different typologies or located in low-income countries, often overlooked by well-established frameworks or a substantial lack of resources.

Mario Santana Quintero

References

Kansa, E. 2022. "The Great Digital Lost and Found: Challenges and Possibilities in Managing Cultural Heritage Data." *Conservation Perspectives: The GCI Newsletter* (online): 4–9. www.getty.edu/conservation/publications_resources/newsletters/pdf/v37n2.pdf

Volk, Michael, Kathryn Frank, and Belinda B. Nettles. 2015. "Managing Coastal Change in the Cultural Landscape: A Case Study in Yankeetown and Inglis, Florida." *Change Over Time* 5 (2): 226–246. https://doi.org/10.1353/cot.2015.0018

Acknowledgements

This research/project was funded by the UK Research and Innovation-Economic and Social Research Council and the Irish Research Council under the 'ESRC-IRC UK/Ireland Networking Grants' (grant numbers ES/V007653/1 and IRC/V007653/1).

The Harbourview project was enabled by the generous donation of time by the communities involved in Wales (Newport Parrog and Porthgain) and Ireland (Ballydehob and Gyles Quay), and the many researchers, engineers, and representatives of government agencies who contributed to the seminar and symposium. These include, in part, in Wales, Dr Julian Whitewright, Susan Fielding, Dr Toby Driver and Scott Lloyd (RCAHMW), Cadw and the NLW; and in Ireland, Barry O'Reilly, Damian Murphy (NIAH) and Colm Murray (Heritage Council). We are also grateful to the local authorities and landowners that facilitated access for the workshops: from Ireland, the Cork and Louth County Councils and in Wales, the Pembrokeshire Coast National Parks Authority, the Barony of Kemaes, and The National Trust.

A special thanks to the volunteers who contributed to the workshops: in Ireland, Julia Barrett, Bill Hastings and Ross Mc Dermott as well SIS Ireland, for donated scanner equipment, and in Wales, Councillor Paul Harries and Reg Atkinson, the Newport Boat Club, Newport Cymdeithas Gychod Afon Nyfer a Harbwr Trefdraeth (Moorings Committee), Professor Luigi Barazzetti (Politecnico di Milano), Stella Rhode, and Jamie Gilchrist.

1 Coastal Heritage, Communities & Climate Change

Elizabeth Shotton

Introduction

Within the context of our rapidly evolving climate, coastal heritage across the world has come under increasing threat as sea levels rise and storms increase in regularity and severity. The situation is particularly acute for small piers and quays, once central to local communities and economies, that have generally fallen into disuse as trade was centralised to major ports. Researchers in coastal studies and heritage, as well as the local and national bodies tasked with their management, have become progressively more concerned about this situation, driving calls for the comprehensive documentation of these structures, as well as sponsoring discussions regarding the long-term viability of conserving this endangered heritage.

The communities living along these coastlines, and deeply attached to their heritage, are facing these threats very directly, often with the sense of having little agency in these discussions or the decisions being taken. Yet they could have a central role to play as first-hand observers of the impact of climate change on their heritage and as partners in documentation and adaptive planning.

The current volume seeks to address this pressing need to document these small piers and quays, the role of communities in this process, and the attendant questions regarding their long-term conservation. Section 1 offers guidance to local and national governments on structuring comprehensive audits of local piers and quays (Chapter 2), analysing and cataloguing the resulting data (Chapter 3), and capturing the potential of digital documentation in their records (Chapter 4). The increase in far more user-friendly and inexpensive methods of 3D recording and visualisation can not only facilitate this documentation effort, as discussed in Chapter 4 but also enable communities to play a more active role in this process. This is illustrated in Section 2 through guidance on the use of these technologies (Chapters 5 and 6) and community-based case studies (Chapters 6 and 7). The various viewpoints regarding the appropriate management and long-term conservation of coastal heritage under threat are reviewed in the Epilogue (Chapter 8) as an aid to further discussion. The collection of essays offers a comprehensive and inclusive overview of

DOI: 10.4324/9781003385097-1

This chapter has been made available under a CC-BY-NC-ND license.

the invaluable role of different participants, working collectively in the active documentation and management of endangered coastal heritage.

Maritime Heritage in Context

Maritime or coastal heritage has been discussed and researched extensively in the fields of maritime archaeology, history, and economics for many decades, as discussed in Chapter 2. While the latter discipline tended to focus on the socio-economic aspects of trade or communities, the limited historical research on the physical structures linking land to sea has generally focused on major port developments or construction technologies, with only modest attention paid to the numerous smaller pier and quay structures that populate the coastlines of Europe and the UK. Thus, records for harbour structures developed and archived by national bodies in Ireland and much of the UK, with the notable exception of Wales (Chapter 4), are both limited and biased in favour of large ports over the far more numerous local piers and quays scattered along the coastline (Chapter 2).

Maritime archaeology would seem to be the discipline best suited to address this knowledge gap. As early as Westerdahl's noteworthy essay of 1992, the maritime cultural landscape was defined as being comprised of 'the whole network of sailing routes, old as well as new, *with ports and harbours along the coast*, and its related constructions and remains of human activity, underwater as well as terrestrial' (Westerdahl 1992; italics added). Westerdahl, a Swedish archaeologist, is a significant figure in this field and it was his survey of the coast of Swedish Norrland in the late 1970s that first coined the phrase maritime cultural landscape. But, as with Westerdahl's work, much of the research emphasis in maritime archaeology has been underwater, on ancient harbours, shipwrecks and fishing weirs, or above water on the study of historic boats and fishing cultures, rather than the infrastructure linking land to sea. The efforts of the historians Gordon Jackson and Adrian Jervis went some way to address this oversight, most particularly Jackson's 2001 'The Significance of Unimportant Ports', which brought much-needed attention to the multitude of small piers and quays along the British coastline (Chapter 3). This was followed up by researchers in Portugal (Amorim 2006), France (Le Bouedec 2009) and, to a lesser degree, in North America (Ford 2011). Yet, these 'unimportant' ports continue to remain largely overlooked, despite calls for their comprehensive documentation in Ireland and Scotland (Chapter 2). The extensive survey of the mainland Scottish harbours by the antiquarian Angus Graham in the mid-20th century (Chapter 3) still stands as the greatest contribution to the documentation of these small but important coastal features in the British Isles. Yet even Graham's immense effort is challenged by Wyatt (Chapter 3) on the grounds of being less than systematic in its methodology and analysis.

Wyatt makes a credible argument for analysing and categorising these small structures in a purpose-built framework that acknowledges the difference between these structures and the better-documented major ports, upon which most taxonomies are founded. These structures have very different relationships to the landscapes in which they are set, the communities they serve, the form adopted based on tides, boats, and uses, as well as often regionally inflected construction methods. It is these factors, in part, which have led to an inconsistency of classification when they are recorded (Chapter 3), as seen in the Irish and Welsh national inventories, reviewed as part of the *Harbourview* (2020–2022) project.

What is especially telling in the Welsh records (Chapter 4) is the inclusion of anchorages and landing places; places with no built interventions that are, nevertheless, critical to understanding the maritime history of a region. If smaller harbour structures are underrepresented in national inventories generally, landing places and anchorages are simply absent with the exception of the Welsh records, despite being recognised by Wyatt (Chapter 3) as part of the maritime heritage that deserves recognition and documentation. This makes the comprehensive recording of landing places in counties Donegal and Galway in the material audits undertaken by the county engineering departments in 1996 and 2001 respectively (Chapter 2) particularly important records, which deserve to find their way into a more public database. Perhaps equally compelling in the story of these audits is the role that engineers, tasked with the maintenance of these structures, could play if drawn into the dialogue on heritage.

As discussed in Chapter 6, minor harbours and landing places have suffered from the same marginalisation as that of industrial heritage, falling outside the scope of the traditional heritage cannon. It is the peripheral nature of these structures, both geographically and thematically, from the idea of what heritage represents in the national ideology (Chapter 8), that has contributed to the under-recording of these structures. The need to reframe the heritage discourse has been recognised in the last 30 years, with landscapes and heritage increasingly understood to be influenced by processes of interaction and change (Chapter 8). This has undoubtedly aided in the increased attention that these small harbours and havens have begun to receive. But it is climate change and its credible impact on coastal areas in Europe that has been a deciding factor in the current calls to document these places (Chapter 2).

The Impact of Climate Change

Climate change has served to refocus the heritage community's attention on the coastline, with damage to the harbour structures having been described by Colm Murray, while working at the Heritage Council in Ireland, as a 'harbinger' of what is to come (email correspondence with author 25 March 2020). As discussed in Chapter 2, both Ireland and Scotland have identified the urgent need to document these historic and culturally important structures more systematically in view of this increased risk. Yet in both jurisdictions, there is an abundance of these structures; Ireland alone has over 900, with several hundred more if the coastline of Northern Ireland was included in this count (Chapter 2). Coastal countries around the globe face similar quandaries regarding their coastal heritage. The sheer numbers involved, and their often-remote locations, make such a call to documentation appear all but impossible to achieve in the coming decades.

As both Prizeman (Chapter 6) and Egberts (Chapter 8) note, there is a need to anticipate the consequences of this rapidly evolving climate, particularly in coastal settings. Naturally, it is the safety and well-being of communities suffering from these impacts that must be addressed with some urgency to create more resilient environments. But the historic maritime structures that gave rise to these settlements, imbuing them with memories of a bygone era of local fishing or trade – of a maritime-based economy – are equally under threat as illustrated by the regular overtopping of piers and quays at high tide. While the high tide in 2014 pictured at Bullock Harbour in Ireland (Figure 1.1) was considered a singular event, the over-topping of the older and lower pier at nearby Sandycove (see Chapter 5) happens at more regular high tides. The situation is particularly extreme in Dublin Bay, where both Bullock and Sandycove are located, where the sea level is rising at twice the global average (6–7 mm/year) according to a 2019 report by Codema (as quoted. in Department 2019, 39). If 7 mm per year does not seem so great, consider that the highest tide at Dublin

Figure 1.1 Bullock Harbour (Ireland) main pier and quay edge overtopped at extraordinary high tide. Photograph by Eamon McElroy, Chief Engineer, Dublin Port, 2014. Reproduced courtesy of the Dublin Port Archive.

will reach the top of the main pier at Bullock in 2023, with high tides regularly overtopping it by 2050 as they currently do at Sandycove. Based on a US Geological Survey study (Doyle, Chivoiu, and Enwright 2015, 16), at the time of Bullock's construction in 1820 (1820), it would have had a comfortable 300 mm or more between high tide and the pier deck, with sea levels only starting to rise in the late 19th century. And though Dublin Bay may be peculiarly impacted, a cursory troll of local Irish newspapers surfaces similar images along a coast experiencing a rise of a mere 3 mm per year (Keogh 2020).

There has been a recognition in research and policy within the heritage sector regarding the need for climate adaptation responses (Department 2019) as discussed in the conversation with Dr Egberts (Chapter 8). While it is widely accepted that coastal environments are the most vulnerable in the immediate term, either from erosion or from flooding, much of the concern in the heritage sector has focused on the disruption of underwater archaeological sites, such as shipwrecks, or national monuments adjacent to eroding coastlines, as witnessed in the significant Irish-Welsh *Climate, Heritage and Environments of Reefs, Islands and Headlands* (CHERISH) research project, which mapped sites such as Dunbeg Fort in County Kerry (Department 2019; Pollard 2020). However, CHERISH has more recently begun to survey harbours in collaboration with the RCAHMW (Chapter 4). Although the climate adaption plan produced in 2019 by the Department of Culture, Heritage, and the Gaeltacht in Ireland certainly identified piers and quays as part of the heritage at risk, there is little mention of how to address them in the report. One suspects that the Department's ambition to assess risk based on 'exposure, sensitivity and adaptive capacity (resilience)', may factor into this oversight. As water-based infrastructural elements, it may be that there is an assumed inherent resilience built into these structures, as described in the 2021 *Fingal Cultural Heritage & Climate Change Risk Assessment* (Land 2021, 42). Yet the rather chilling image from Bullock Harbour in 2014 (Figure 8.1) should worry not only heritage officers and county engineers but also those tasked with coastal safety, as the overtopping of these structures with increasing frequency will render them hazardous to both pedestrians and boating traffic. This alone demands an intersectoral response, as advised in the Department's report and echoed by Egberts (Chapter 8).

Coupled with the impact of sea level rise is the future damage likely to occur, driven by the increase in mean wave heights (0.8 m per decade on Irish shores) and the number and intensity of storms increasing at a rate of 3 per decade in the Atlantic since 1950 (Department 2019, 19). This puts the engineers tasked with the maintenance of these structures in an unenviable position, likely requiring more funds than may be available. Departments such as this already face overwhelming odds in the ongoing maintenance of local piers and quays, many privately built, which once enabled trade and fishing to thrive in remote locations but are now largely unused. Despite the presumed resilience of such structures, the engineers tasked with their maintenance are all too well aware of how quickly they can fall into a state of

Figure 1.2 Minihane's Quay, Ballydehob, County Cork, Ireland. Photograph by Elizabeth Shotton, 2021.

disrepair (Figure 1.2) without constant oversight. As Whitewright (Chapter 4) and Prizeman (Chapter 6) rightly advise, documentation efforts are critical in order to, at a minimum, ensure the preservation of these structures by the record in the event of major loss or damage, as is being done by projects such as CHERISH, CITiZAN (Chapter 4) and the online mapping of coastal sites at risk by *The SCAPE Trust* in Scotland (SCAPE n.d.).

The capacity to undertake such a significant task of documentation rapidly has improved in light of the evolution of low-cost digital survey technologies as discussed by Prizeman (Chapter 6) and Whitewright (Chapter 4). This is true not only for the work of institutions such as the RCAHMW (Chapter 4) but also for local community efforts as at Ballydehob, County Cork (Chapter 7) and Newport Parrog in Wales (Chapter 6). Given the immediacy of the risk to these structures and the scale of the documentation effort required (Chapter 2), empowering local communities to participate in these efforts may prove imperative.

The Potential of Community Participation

In the past decade there has been considerable effort made by researchers to engage with communities on archaeology projects (Johnston and Marwood 2017; Ounanian et al. 2021) following the adoption of the *Faro Convention on the Value of Cultural Heritage for Society* with its emphasis on involving 'everyone in society in the ongoing process of defining and managing cultural heritage' (Council 2005, 1). These efforts have been mirrored in several recent Irish-Welsh coastal research projects such as CHERISH, CCAT, *Ports, Past & Present*, and the *Harbourview* project (2020–22); the CITiZAN project in England; the SCAPE project in Scotland; and the earlier European-wide *Hericoast* project, which investigated participatory models of governance for heritage. The rationale for participatory management of coastal heritage (Ounanian et al. 2021, 1), echoed by Egberts (Chapter 8), as part of a regional governance policy, is becoming increasingly compelling given the pressing timeframe for documentation and future planning.

Many of these projects fostered community engagement through online mapping projects (*Ports, Past & Present*) or climate adaptation workshops (CCAT) rather than relying on communities to undertake documentation. However, as illustrated in the community-based case study in Ballydehob (Chapter 7), undertaken as part of *Harbourview*, the local populace can act as a driving force in both documenting and helping to conserve these structures, particularly given the recent advent of inexpensive 3D digital recording technologies as discussed in Chapters 5 and 6. There has been resistance to community-led documentation efforts, which have largely centred around questions of accuracy (Fitton et al. 2021, 5). While there may be merit to this argument, there were a surprising amount of specialist skills found among the Ballydehob community (Chapter 7) that belie these concerns.

Though the skills found in Ballydehob are unlikely to be found in every local community, Hastings (Chapter 5) provides very useful guidance to communities on how to approach simple methods of documentation such as sketching and deliberate photography. The usefulness of the latter technique is clearly demonstrated in Kevin O'Farrell's careful photographic documentation of the details of Ballydehob Quay which served to reveal details otherwise overlooked (Chapter 7). In addition to other avenues for documentation that require far less specialist knowledge, Hastings also provides advice on selecting the appropriate methods based on skill level as does the recently published CHERISH Toolkit (link in Resources for Communities). The Ballydehob community itself, recognising the unique composition of its team, suggested that a broader regional approach could be used, with neighbouring communities sharing their expertise to document multiple harbours in their locale (Chapter 7).

Even a simple photographic survey linked to a *Google Earth* map can serve as a baseline for further documentation efforts. Gleesk harbour, County Kerry (Figure 1.3) was but one of 57 harbours in the county surveyed by Kerry resident Michael O'Carroll. Having worked as a Harbour Master in Kerry, O'Carroll, like many associated with these small harbours, had developed an interest and affection for them, which drove him to document as many as he could locate on the Kerry coastline. His example speaks to the potential of communities to work with their local councils to document these historic structures before they succumb to damage inflicted by a changing climate.

8 *Elizabeth Shotton*

Figure 1.3 Gleesk Harbour, County Kerry. Photograph by Michael O'Carroll, 2009.

Local communities could also serve as on-site observers of the incremental impacts of climate change at their harbours, which could be capitalised on by regional or national bodies tasked with recording or maintaining these structures. This form of crowd-sourced monitoring has been formalised by Parks Canada and the University of Windsor in their *Coastie* initiative (https://coastiecanada.ca/), where mobile phone cradles were installed in specific locations at coastal sites to gather photographic data to monitor coastal erosion, inspired by *CoastSnap* that began in Australia in 2017. Informal monitoring is already taking place by communities threatened by climate impacts in Ireland and the UK as evident in the Facebook pages of *Save Bulloch* and the *Aberaeron Flood Reaction Group* in Wales. Yet, without coordination, these potentially valuable records will be lost. The system of allowing 'events' to be recorded on the *Canmore* database (https://canmore.org.uk/contributions), as described by McKeague and Thomas (2016, 117) 'paved the way for enabling the public to contribute information and images directly to the database', which may illustrate a means of capturing the input of local communities as well as researchers.

But it is not simply the need for documentation that engagement with local communities can address. As evidenced by the material audits undertaken in Ireland (Chapter 2), engagement with the community can unearth local knowledge that would simply be unavailable to specialists surveying these sites. In the case of the material audits, it was the locales of unbuilt landing places, while for Ballydehob it was knowledge of the relationship between the main quay at Ballydehob and the multiple satellite quays, many privately owned, in the bay.

Engaging with local communities to document these historic harbours requires a closer alliance and effective communication between regional and national bodies tasked with maintaining these records and the communities that could contribute to them. Communities need to understand how to structure their efforts, to ensure that information is gathered in a form that can be integrated with official inventories (Chapter 2). Equally, national and regional coordination is necessary to ensure that efforts are not duplicated, and that data is archived and shared effectively (Chapters 4 and 7). As the Ballydehob community clearly articulated (Chapter 7), their efforts are in vain without a regional or national framework set up to govern, facilitate, and archive such work.

Conclusion

The accelerated impacts of climate change, by virtue of putting these small harbour structures at serious risk, have increased awareness of their largely undocumented status. Simultaneously, the proliferation of low-cost digital documentation techniques has provided tools to address this need for rapid documentation. While there is still a need for specialist expertise in some scenarios (Chapter 6), there is an opportunity to harness the passion local communities have for their harbours by engaging them in this process of documentation. Yet, there remain a number of areas to address to achieve coherent inventories of these structures.

The contemporary heritage classification systems need to develop more appropriate frameworks for analysis specific to these types of structures, as argued by Wyatt (Chapter 3), with an enlargement of the types of information they traditionally collect and maintain to include harbour-specific data such as tidal ranges and deck levels (Chapter 2). There is also an overlooked potential of the role that local engineering departments could play in developing and maintaining these inventories, given their regular oversight of these structures (Chapter 2). While enabling successful community participation in this effort requires a reconsideration of how regional and national authorities, tasked with collecting and maintaining these records, interact with local communities (Chapter 7).

There are also other questions about developing appropriate climate adaptation strategies for such structures that are, as yet, largely unaddressed. As argued by DeSilvey (2017), our attitude toward the preservation of heritage may need to evolve to accept some level of loss (Chapter 8). With such a large inventory of coastal heritage under threat, difficult choices may be required as to how much should be saved, and at what cost. This knowledge makes the recording of these vulnerable structures all the more pressing. But it also reinforces the need for community engagement in this process, as local communities may be best positioned to help inform these difficult decisions. This type of participatory governance to address climate adaptation was the subject of an international study by Fitton et al. (2021, 6), which concluded that these small communities may well have strategic advantages in adaptability. There was evidence that consensus could be achieved more readily in small communities regarding adaptation planning supported through the use of 3D visualisations. This argues for a closer working relationship between government agencies, researchers and local communities on the documentation and forward planning of their maritime heritage.

References

Amorim, I. 2006. "Portuguese Free Ports at the Turn of the Eighteenth Century: A Strategy to Promote "Unimportant" Ports." *International Journal of Maritime History* 18 (1): 103–128.

Council of Europe. 2005. *Council of Europe Framework Convention on the Value of Cultural Heritage for Society. Council of Europe Treaty Series No. 199*. Faro: Council of Europe. https://rm.coe.int/1680083746

Department of Culture, Heritage, and the Gaeltacht. 2019. *Built & Archaeological Heritage: Climate Change Sectoral Adaptation Plan*. Dublin: Government of Ireland.

DeSilvey, C. 2017. *Curated Decay: Heritage Beyond Saving*. Minneapolis: University of Minnesota Press.

Doyle, Thomas, Bogdan Chivoiu, and Nicholas Enwright. 2015. "Sea-Level Rise Modeling Handbook: Resource Guide for Coastal Land Managers, Engineers, and Scientists." Professional Paper 1815, U.S. Geological Survey, Reston. http://dx.doi.org/10.3133/pp1815

Fitton, J. M., et al. 2021. "Challenges to Climate Change Adaptation in Coastal Small Towns: Examples from Ghana, Uruguay, Finland, Denmark, and Alaska." *Ocean & Coastal Management* 212: 105787.

Ford, B., ed. 2011. *The Archaeology of Maritime Landscapes. When the Land Meets the Sea*. New York: Springer.

Jackson, G. 2001. "The Significance of Unimportant Ports." *International Journal of Maritime History* 13 (2): 1–17.

Johnston, R., and K. Marwood. 2017. "Action Heritage: Research, Communities, Social Justice." *International Journal of Heritage Studies* 23 (9): 816–831.

Keogh, J. 2020. "Wet, Wet, WET! West Cork Counts Cost of Third Major Flood in a Fortnight." *The Southern Star*. August 31st, 2020.

Land Use Consultants Ltd. 2021. *Fingal Cultural Heritage & Climate Change Risk Assessment Fingal: Fingal County Council*. www.fingal.ie/fingal-cultural-heritage-climate-change-risk-assessment

Le Bouedec, G., 2009. "Small Ports from the Sixteenth to the Early Twentieth Century and the Local Economy of the French Atlantic Coast." *International Journal of Maritime History* XXI (2): 103–126.

McKeague, Peter, and David Thomas. 2016. "Evolution of National Heritage Inventories for Scotland and Wales." *Journal of Cultural Heritage Management and Sustainable Development* 6 (2): 113–127. https://doi.org/10.1108/JCHMSD-01-2016-0003

Ounanian, K., et al. 2021. "Conceptualizing Coastal and Maritime Cultural Heritage through Communities of Meaning and Participation." *Ocean & Coastal Management* 212: 105806.

Pollard, E. 2020. "The Crumbling Promontory Fort of Dunbeg." In *CHERISH*. Ireland and Wales: CHERISH. Accessed January 2023. http://cherishproject.eu/en/project-news/blog-posts/the-crumbling-promontory-fort-of-dunbeg/

SCAPE. n.d. "Sites at Risk." In *The SCAPE Trust*. St Andrews: St Andrews University and Historic Scotland. https://scapetrust.org/sites-at-risk/

Westerdahl, C. 1994. "The Maritime Cultural Landscape." *The International Journal of Nautical Archaeology* 21 (1): 5–14.

Section 1
Inventories, Classifications & Management

2 Inventories of Maritime Heritage

Elizabeth Shotton

Introduction

The systematic inventorying of historic buildings, monuments, sea wrecks, designed landscapes, or piers and quays is essential to establishing what exists, describing what condition it is in, evaluating its historical worth, and determining which should be granted some form of statutory protection. These surveys can also be used to identify what may be at risk of deterioration or demolition, therefore requiring more immediate attention, described as a risk register. Such inventories are most often funded and maintained by national government bodies, though regional governments also play a role in certain countries.

Inventories can be as simple as identifying locations, as was done for ancient monuments in the early Ordnance Surveys in Ireland and the UK in the early 19th century. These typically had descriptive notes affiliated with them in the field books carried by surveyors and would, on occasion, draw on information from other sources, as was documented in the letter books of the first Ordnance Survey in Ireland. Current inventories by government bodies, be they regional or national, tend to be more elaborate but are still founded on the same principle of first knowing what exists and where it is located in order to effectively manage these assets (Myers 2016, 102). This may include creating records not for conservation efforts but as a means to remember what had existed should it disappear. The creation of the initial location data and descriptive record acts as the base from which further sources can be drawn and evaluations made (Illsley 2023, 2). This can include other documents or archival records, photographs, and on-site drawings. More recently the increasing use of 3D digital models from Lidar scans or drone surveys by archaeologists and other researchers can sometimes be added to the record.

A more systematic framework for recording heritage was established in the UK in the early 20th century with the founding of the Royal Commissions in Scotland, Wales and England. In Ireland, though the 1930s National Monument Act served to give some protection to pre-1700 heritage, it was the foundation of the Archaeological Services in the 1960s that established a consistent system of surveys, inventories, and record-keeping. The work of the Archaeological Services covers monuments that pre-date 1700 (with some exceptions) which are recorded in a Sites and Monuments Record (SMR). In response to the Granada Convention of 1985, the Irish National Inventory of Architectural Heritage (NIAH) was established in 1990 with a remit to record a representative sample of built works post-1700 (Hamond and McMahon 2002, 4; NIAH 2023b, 4). Local County Councils in Ireland also maintain Records of Protected Structures (RPS), which differ from the NIAH surveys as they offer statutory protection.

The scope of these inventories has gradually expanded from ancient monuments, such as hill forts or cairns, to historic buildings and, more recently in Ireland, to gardens. The recording of industrial heritage, such as mines or bridges, while present on both the National Monuments and the NIAH inventories, was considered inconsistent in its coverage (Hamond and McMahon 2002, 12), leading to the Heritage Council (Ireland) sponsored publication *Recording and Conserving Ireland's Industrial Heritage: An Introductory Guide* in 2002. This is a very useful document for local communities or groups to refer to in undertaking a survey of their own heritage, regardless of whether it is industrial in nature, as it provides simple guidance on how to plan for and structure such an endeavour (Figure 2.1). And for harbour enthusiasts, it is gratifying to see piers and quays in their list of industrial sites. Yet, despite references in this useful guidance document, piers and quays remain under-surveyed in Ireland by the heritage community, a situation that has also been highlighted in Scotland. The Scottish Archaeological Research Framework (ScARF) has noted that 'this extensive resource has thus far only been subjected to limited ad hoc study and there is a case for a broader, more integrated approach to harbour research' in the future (ScARF n.d.).

In this context, the material condition audits of local piers, quays and landing places, sponsored by the then Department for Arts, Heritage, Gaeltacht, and the Islands in Ireland in the late 1990s are remarkable for their scope, of great historical value, and a useful case study for future inventories of maritime heritage.

Inventories of Piers, Quays and Landing Places: An Irish Case Study

An inventory of heritage engineering works (HEW) maintained by Trinity College Dublin and published in Cox and Gould's 1998 *Ireland: Civil Engineering Heritage* (updated in 2013) represented an early attempt to record some harbour works. This is mirrored in the UK by HEW records collected and maintained by the Institution of Civil Engineers (ICE), though neither seems to be linked to national heritage databases. In both cases, the interest was in major ports rather than the far more numerous local piers and quays. In Ireland, harbours conventionally fall into one of three categories: commercial ports managed by dedicated semi-state companies, such as Dublin Port Company; commercial fishing ports identified by the Department of Agriculture, Food and the Marine; and,

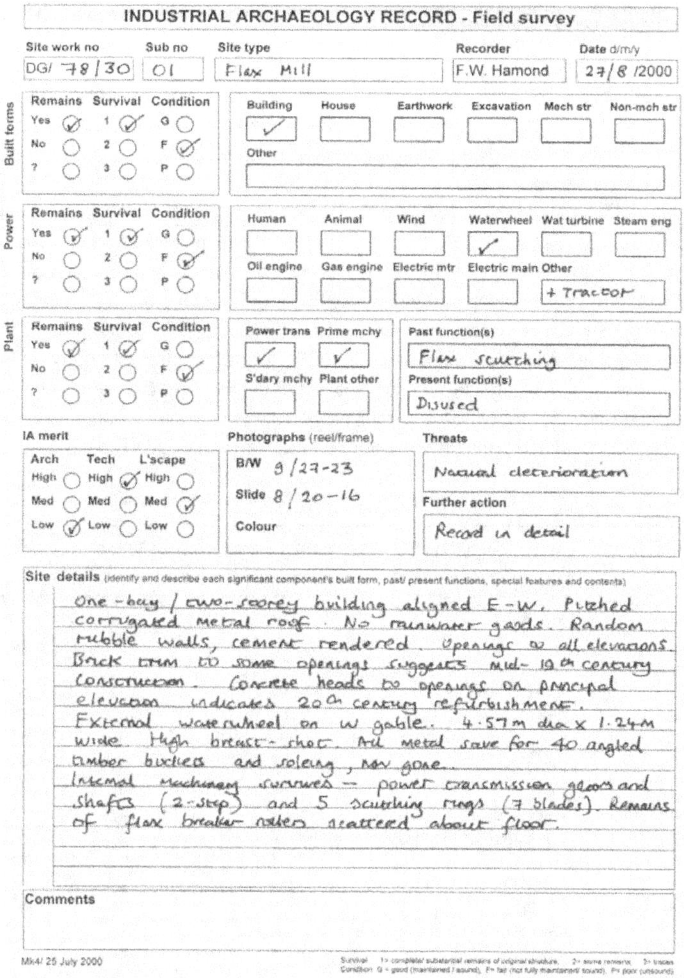

INDUSTRIAL ARCHAEOLOGY RECORD - Field survey

Site work no: DG/ 78/30 | Sub no: 01 | Site type: Flax Mill | Recorder: F.W. Hamond | Date d/m/y: 27/8/2000

Built forms — Remains: Yes ✓ | Survival: 1 ✓ | Condition: F ✓ — Building ✓; House; Earthwork; Excavation; Mech str; Non-mch str; Other

Power — Remains: Yes ✓ | Survival: 1 ✓ | Condition: F ✓ — Human; Animal; Wind; Waterwheel ✓; Wat turbine; Steam eng; Oil engine; Gas engine; Electric mtr; Electric main; Other: + Tractor

Plant — Remains: Yes ✓ | Survival: 1 ✓ | Condition: F ✓ — Power trans ✓; Prime mchy ✓; S'dary mchy; Plant other

Past function(s): Flax scutching

Present function(s): Disused

IA merit — Arch: Low ✓ | Tech: High ✓ | L'scape: Med ✓

Photographs (reel/frame) — B/W: 9/27-23; Slide: 8/20-16; Colour

Threats: Natural deterioration

Further action: Record in detail

Site details (identify and describe each significant component's built form, past/ present functions, special features and contents)

One-bay / two-storey building aligned E-W. Pitched corrugated metal roof. No rainwater goods. Random rubble walls, cement rendered. Openings on all elevations. Brick trim to some openings suggests mid-19th century construction. Concrete heads to openings on principal elevation indicates 20th century refurbishment. External waterwheel on W gable. 4.57m dia x 1.24m wide. High breast-shot. All metal save for 40 angled timber buckets and soleing, now gone. Internal machinery survives – power transmission gears and shafts (2-step) and 5 scutching rings (7 blades). Remains of flax breaker rollers scattered about floor.

Comments

Mk4/ 25 July 2000

Figure 2.1 Sample template for an inventory from *Recording and Conserving Ireland's Industrial Heritage: An Introductory Guide* (Hamond and McMahon 2002).

most numerous of all, the small piers and quays used locally for fishing, seaweed harvesting, transport or recreation. The small piers and quays are typically privately owned or under the authority of the local council and were in 1995 estimated to be in excess of 900 (Dáil 1995). It is these minor structures that ScARF referred to in calling for a more integrated approach to research, and which are common to all European coastlines. These are also the structures most threatened by climate change due to their reduced use, which has made it difficult to rationalise the commitment of funds to their maintenance. As the team at ScARF has noted, this threat is then 'compounded by the poor levels of recording that have prevailed in this sector' (ScARF n.d.).

While there are piers, quays and other maritime infrastructure along the sea coast listed on the National Monuments database (96 SMR records) and the NIAH database (148 records for coastal counties), they are, as with the industrial heritage, unsystematic in their coverage (National 2023; NIAH 2023a). Since the SMR coverage principally represents archaeological ruins, it is not comparable to the estimate of current local piers and quays. However, it is worth noting that 34 of the 96 records relate to Dublin city centre, indicative of the bias in coverage. While the NIAH records are only intended to be representative, rather than comprehensive, and the county Record of Protected Status (RPS) are likewise only used to protect piers and quays considered to have heritage significance, the unevenness of the records relative to the estimated quantity of local piers and quays in each county suggests that more systematic and comprehensive inventories are required (Table 2.1).

Table 2.1 Local Piers, Quays and Landing Places on the Irish Coastline

Location	Coastal Counties	No. of Piers & Quays[1]	NIAH[2]	RPS[2]
West	Donegal	155	17	1
West	Sligo	10	6	6
West	Mayo	78	15	1
West	Galway	244	45	33
West	Clare	71	4	19
West	Kerry	58	0	1
West	Limerick	30	6	4
South	Cork	207	20	1
South	Waterford	15	14	3
East	Dun Laoghaire Rathdown	7	0	9[3]
East	Fingal	9	6	9[3]
East	Louth	9	4	4
East	Wicklow	4	0	0
East	Wexford	15	11	1
	Total	**912**	**148**	**92**

1. Preliminary estimates based on lists from county engineers coupled with Ordnance Survey map analysis. The preliminary estimate excludes major harbours maintained by Port companies (Dublin, Foynes, Cork, Waterford, New Ross, Drogheda, Dundalk, Galway) and structures in ruin.
2. Excludes major harbours maintained by Port companies (Dublin, Foynes, Cork, Waterford, New Ross, Drogheda, Dundalk, Galway) including extensive records for Dublin quays.
3. Dun Laoghaire Rathdown (DLR), as with other counties, often identifies single piers in their RPS that, as a collection, form a single harbour. Thus, one harbour (Dun Laoghaire) has four RPS records, creating a situation where RPS records exceed the number of harbours. There are at least two harbours in DLR which are not on the RPS. This duplication also occurs in Howth and Rush harbours in Fingal.

Inventories of Maritime Heritage 19

Yet comprehensive inventories of local piers, quays and landing places do exist in Ireland. Counties Donegal, Galway, and Mayo all undertook extensive surveys in 1996, 2001 and 2004 respectively. These were not undertaken within the framework of the heritage system in Ireland but instead were sponsored by the then Department for Arts, Heritage, Gaeltacht, and the Islands to assess the conditions of piers and quays in order to identify four piers within the Gaeltacht regions (Irish speaking; see Figure 2.2) in each county for further funding and development (Waters 2022). Given their intended use, these audits were undertaken by the county engineering departments which have

Figure 2.2 Map of Gaeltacht regions (shaded in grey) in Ireland c. 2015. Drawn by author from data from the Marine Irish Digital Atlas (http://mida.ucc.ie/pages/atlas/atlas.php).

responsibility for maintaining these structures, often through the agency of consulting engineering firms (Ryan 2001). The result was a series of lengthy and carefully executed material condition audits of even the smallest structures, including unbuilt natural landing places, complete with maps, notes, photographs and, in many cases, drawings. Though the original audits are now above 20 years out of date, some county engineering departments continue to update them following maintenance works.

At the same time, in 1997, a national inventory of piers and harbours was commenced by the Underwater Archaeology Unit (UAU) of the National Monuments Service (Underwater 2002; Heritage 2006, 59). This document, though unpublished, is available to be reviewed on request and is very useful to maritime researchers despite its limitations. The survey in this case was a desk-based review of the Office of Public Works (OPW) records, the organisation which had built many of the local piers in Ireland in the 19th century. Unfortunately, the OPW records are not complete, and though their annual reports fill in much of the missing information, even a full record of OPW-built works represents no more than half of the local piers and quays along the coastline, missing locally built quays such as Ballydehob and its satellite quays. Nor does it establish whether the structure is still extant or, in some cases, whether it was ever built.

In contrast to the UAU survey, the material audits in the western counties resulted in more than half of the local Irish harbours, including unbuilt landing places, having been carefully documented. By 2006 the Heritage Council, also under the remit of the Department for Arts, Heritage, Gaeltacht, and the Islands, made a further call for the documentation of these structures (Heritage 2006, 58–60), which sponsored a similarly comprehensive audit of maritime heritage in county Clare in 2008 by their heritage and conservation officers (Halpin and O'Connor 2008). Thus, despite the unevenness of the national records and the county RPS lists, these four inventories provide systematic and comprehensive records for an estimated 60% of local piers and quays in Ireland. Unfortunately, with the exception of the Clare inventory and a smaller but similar study in Fingal (John 2010), much of this information is inaccessible to the public, and thus its existence is largely unknown even, in some cases, to the heritage and conservation officers of these counties. Yet they serve as a useful template for other local or regional authorities in Ireland and beyond Irish shores for use in identifying and recording their coastal heritage in a systematic fashion.

Types of Data Collected

Identifying and locating these structures is the first step common to an inventory. In Ireland, the local county engineers tasked with maintaining these small piers and quays are often the best people to look to for information.

Although many of these small structures are privately owned, in practice most counties will have a record of them and maintain them if they are on a public route. From there, the type of information documented varies depending on the reason for the inventory (Hamond and McMahon 2002, 13). In the case of the material condition audits by the county engineering departments, it was driven by the ambition to identify the most likely piers for further development, and thus covered a range of salient topics unlikely to be found in a heritage inventory:

- ownership
- use (fishing, recreation, tourist, etc.) and volume (the number of boats)
- distance to a nearest population centre
- plan sketch of the pier
- photographs of the pier, overview and detailing any damage
- access details (private, public, cul-de-sac, etc.)
- details on parking accommodation
- pier structure (configuration, dimensions, material, depth of water at the time of survey, type of deck material, type of moorings, damage)
- heritage value
- safety (guard rails, life buoys, etc.)
- amenities (lighting, electricity, signage, water supply, toilets)
- slipway
- dredging requirement
- sea access (how often does it dry out)
- and berthage (also related to tides)

In most cases, these criteria were given a ranking, in an effort to create a shortlist of the piers with the greatest potential for further development. Deterioration or damage was also carefully documented, and cost estimates made for repairs, the latter best left to consulting engineers. These records were recently made public, in abbreviated form (Figure 2.3), on the Galway County Open Data Portal (Galway 2016).

While much of this data may seem incidental to a heritage survey, the wealth of information in these documents is of significance not only to engineers but also to researchers. Noel Wilkins, author of Humble Works for Humble People (2017), had already significantly progressed this work by the time he was given access to this inventory in 2002. But Wilkins acknowledged that it highlighted piers he had been unaware of and that its extensive detail allowed him to describe the piers more accurately (email correspondence, June 2023). Equally, seemingly small details such as the depth of water at a certain date and time – critical to an engineer accessing the viability of berthage and sea access – could provide essential historical data for estimating sea level changes due to climate change.

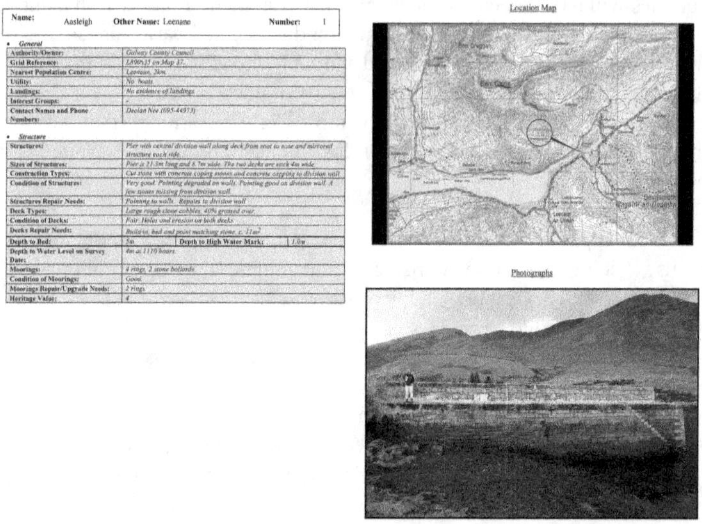

22 *Elizabeth Shotton*

Figure 2.3 Partial record for Aasleigh Pier, County Galway from *Piers, Harbours, and Landing Places of Galway County* (Galway 2016, with permission of Galway County Council)

What these audits lack is made clear in the Clare Coastal Survey of 2008 (Figure 2.4). Though containing far less information on material condition, depth of water, and current use, this survey fills in the historical background to the structures, drawing on other sources such as the OPW files and annual reports, and providing a provisional date of construction.

There are lessons to be taken from both these surveys, most obviously that the reasons for the inventory will drive the detail that is collected, and hence should be established from the outset (Hamond and McMahon 2002, 13). As Hamond and McMahon illustrate in their useful categorisation of the four levels of inventory types (2002, 14–17), much of the detail acquired in the Galway audit falls into the 4th stage, which they describe would "only be required in exceptional circumstances, for example, site conservation, replication or restoration." Or, in the case of these audits, essential for estimating development potential and probable expense, much of which could only be undertaken by a specialist. In contrast, the Clare survey addressed levels 1 and 2, providing a general description of the structure through location data, site photographs, and references to public documents, which established what deserved to be recorded in greater detail. But in the case of maritime heritage recording, particularly in a time of rapid climate change, water depths seem to warrant being captured even in a simple survey to establish what exists, as it will give some indication of its vulnerability to rising sea levels.

Inventories of Maritime Heritage 23

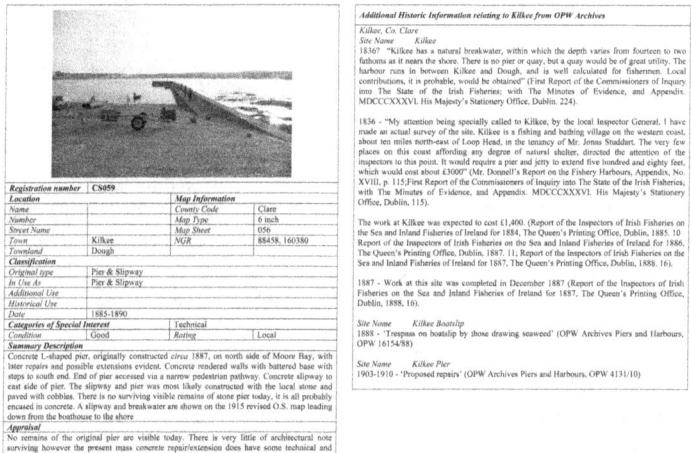

Figure 2.4 Published record for Kilkee Pier from *Clare Coastal Architectural Heritage Survey* (Halpin and O'Connor 2008, with permission of Clare County Council)

Community Engagement

As Illsley has argued, the trajectory of how heritage inventories have developed in the UK, as well as Ireland, 'established the specialist's role interpreting what does or does not belong in the inventory, risking the omission of local knowledge and cultural association with the site or monument' (2023, 2). The Clare survey was undertaken by the county conservation and heritage officers, well versed in the particulars of how to assess the structure's historical value in terms of categories of special interest (architectural, social, technological, etc.) and rating of significance (national, regional, etc.) in line with NIAH guidelines (NIAH 2023b, 16–20). Likewise, much of the material audit undertaken by Galway would require engineering skills to make assessments such as the cost to repair damage. The heritage assessments assigned by the engineers were more impenetrable in their derivation, though they appear to have prioritised piers for preservation based on the quality of their stonework and the novel structural features – thus ranking Aasleigh (Figure 2.3) as the highest priority despite its lack of use (Ryan 2001, 67). Despite the need for these specialist skills, a very unique situation developed in the course of the Galway audit, and likely the Donegal audit before it, that deserves some discussion in light of Illsley's warning regarding the loss of local knowledge due to an overreliance on specialists.

As the Galway audit progressed in early 2000 the engineers at Ryan Hanley found themselves overwhelmed with the scale of the task they had taken on (Waters 2022). It was then that they brought in Hugh Haughey, an engineer who had previously worked with Donegal County Council and who may well have been the author of the Donegal audit in 1996. The reason for this provisional attribution is that both Galway and Donegal included landing places such as unimproved coves or beaches in these audits. This was by no means on the initial brief for these surveys, as the original intention was to identify existing piers for improvement. But Haughey successfully argued for the inclusion of these places in the Galway audit, resulting in a unique inventory of landing places. While in Galway this only amounts to 13 out of 244 entries, with another 4 identified but not surveyed (Ryan 2001, 62), in the case of Donegal landing places made up a third of the sites surveyed (email correspondence with Donegal Engineering Department). This in itself is a significant contribution to the historical record of these counties, as unimproved havens would have been very commonly used for centuries and yet would have little chance of being recorded due to the lack of any built intervention. The identification of these sites would also have required engaging closely with the local populace and, as Waters describes, Haughey was a Gaeilgoir (Irish speaker) enabling him to acquire anecdotal information socially that an English speaker would not (Waters 2022).

While neither survey directly employed local communities in the work as both, in different ways, relied on specialist knowledge, the engagement with the Irish-speaking local communities in Galway and Donegal on the material audits expanded the wealth of information finally recorded in ways that would not have otherwise been possible. As McKeague and Thomas have argued, local communities can add value to such an inventory, inaccessible to the specialist, by virtue of their knowledge of local landmarks, history, and associations (2016, 123).

Conclusion

Though a considerable portion of the local piers and quays on Ireland's west coast have been comprehensively recorded by local authorities, much of it has operated outside of the national bodies responsible for maintaining heritage inventories, and thus beyond the reach of the public or researchers. While the detail on the material audits is compelling, offering insights on features that should be documented for maritime structures beyond the NIAH guidelines, the format of the data, even if transferred to the NIAH, may be difficult to integrate within their system. This suggests that the NIAH may need to incorporate a different range of data fields into their carefully structured system to adequately reflect key characteristics of these structures, such as water depth and benchmark elevations of the pier deck. It is also crucial to develop a shared vocabulary, so everyone knows what a *landing place* is, or what constitutes a *pier* versus a *breakwater, quay or jetty*, the definitions for which vary between regions and cultures. But it also makes clear that inventories undertaken by regional authorities, academic researchers or community-based projects, should be developed in a manner that the data can be easily shared with local and national bodies that have roles in the management of historical records (Carlisle and Lee 2016, 133). McKeague and Thomas go so far as to state that *any* activities documenting the historic environment should be required to contribute their data to the recognised inventories of their region or country (2016, 113).

This issue of the interchange of data is further complicated for records on local piers and quays which often fall under the remit of the engineering departments of local or regional governing bodies operating outside of the heritage and conservation network of specialists. In Ireland, these departments are certainly best placed to evaluate and maintain records of these structures due to their remit to maintain them. Carlisle and Lee (2016, 134) have suggested, with reference to the Historic England records, that the records which are currently held nationally may be better placed with regional authorities who make the most active use of this data, while the national body would be responsible for establishing common data standards and providing digital access. It is a position that could serve well for inventories of local piers and quays which are continuously being transformed through maintenance works by the regional engineering departments.

All of this suggests that a more conscious and coordinated working relationship is needed between these groups, as well as with researchers and local communities to draw in their particular knowledge. The National Monuments Service regularly collects and archives archaeological site reports from professional archaeologists, an important capture of information, which could be replicated at the NIAH. And while the network of conservation and heritage officers across Ireland are well versed in the NIAH survey requirements, in the case of piers and quays it is the engineering departments which should be drawn into a closer operating relationship with the NIAH, as well as the consulting engineers hired to work on these structures.

References

Carlisle, Philip, and Edmund Lee. 2016. "Recording the Past: Heritage Inventories in England." *Journal of Cultural Heritage Management and Sustainable Development* 6: 128–137. https://doi.org/10.1108/JCHMSD-02-2016-0013

Cox, Ronald, and Michael Gould. 1998. *Ireland: Civil Engineering Heritage*. London: Institute of Civil Engineers (ICE).

Dáil Eireann. 1995. "Ceisteanna – Questions. Oral Answers. – Coastal and Island Pier Facilities." In 27th Dáil Debate – Thursday, 18 May 1995. Dublin: Houses of the Oireachtas. https://www.oireachtas.ie/en/debates/debate/dail/1995-05-18/

Galway County Council. 2016. "Piers and Harbours of Galway County." *Galway Open Data Portal*. https://opendata-galwaycoco.hub.arcgis.com/datasets/galwaycoco::piers-and-harbours-of-galway-county/about

Halpin, Sarah, and Gráinne O'Connor. 2008. *Clare Coastal Architectural Heritage Survey/Taighde Oidhreacht Ailtireachta Cósta an Chláir*. Ennis: Clare County Council. www.clarecoco.ie/services/planning/publications/heritageconservation/clare-coastal-architectural-heritage-survey-2008-3752.pdf

Hamond, Fred, and Mary McMahon. 2002. *Recording and Conserving Ireland's Industrial Heritage: An Introductory Guide*. Kilkenny: The Heritage Council. www.heritagecouncil.ie/content/files/recording_conserving_irelands_industrial_heritage_guide_2002_8mb.pdf

Heritage Council (Ireland). 2006. *Conserving Ireland's Maritime Heritage*. Kilkenny: The Heritage Council. www.heritagecouncil.ie/content/files/conserving_irelands_maritime_heritage_2006_2mb.pdf

Illsley, William R. 2023. "Hybrids and Heritage Resources: Rethinking the Social Foundation of Historic Environment Records in England." *Journal of Cultural Heritage Management and Sustainable Development* (ahead-of-print). https://doi.org/10.1108/JCHMSD-09-2022-0154

John Cronin & Associates. 2010. *Fingal Coastal Architectural Heritage Project*. Fingal: Fingal County Council. www.fingal.ie/sites/default/files/2019-04/Fingal%20Coastal%20Architecture%20Study.pdf

McKeague, Peter, and David Thomas. 2016. "Evolution of National Heritage Inventories for Scotland and Wales." *Journal of Cultural Heritage Management and Sustainable Development* 6: 113–127. https://doi.org/10.1108/JCHMSD-01-2016-0003

Myers, David. 2016. "Heritage Inventories: Promoting Effectiveness as a Vital Tool for Sustainable Heritage Management." *Journal of Cultural Heritage Management and Sustainable Development* 6: 102–112. https://doi.org/10.1108/JCHMSD-02-2016-0009

National Monuments Service. 2023. *National Monuments Service – Archaeological Survey of Ireland Dataset*. Ireland: Department of Housing, Local Government, and Heritage. https://data.gov.ie/dataset/national-monuments-service-archaeological-survey-of-ireland?package_type=dataset

NIAH. 2023a. *National Inventory of Architectural Heritage (NIAH) National Dataset*. Ireland: Department of Housing, Local Government, and Heritage. https://data.gov.ie/dataset/national-inventory-of-architectural-heritage-niah-national-dataset?package_type=dataset

NIAH. 2023b. *National Inventory of Architectural Heritage Handbook*. Dublin: National Inventory of Architectural Heritage (NIAH). www.buildingsofireland.ie/app/uploads/2023/04/NIAH-Handbook-Edition-April-2023.pdf

Ryan Hanley Engineers. 2001. *Piers, Harbours, and Landing Places of Galway County*. Vol. 4. Galway: Galway County Council (Unpublished).

ScARF. n.d. "Havens and Harbours." In *Maritime and Marine: Coastal Intertidal and Maritime Hinterland*. Scottish Archaeological Research Framework (ScARF). Accessed 7 September, 2020. https://scarf.scot/thematic/scarf-marine-maritime-panel-report/3-coastal-intertidal-and-maritime-hinterland/3-3-previous-and-current-coastal-intertidal-and-maritime-hinterland-archaeological-research-projects-in-scotland/3-3-3-subject-area-research/havens-and-harbours/

Underwater Archaeology Unit. 2002. *Piers, Ports and Harbours: Draft Inventory in 2 Volumes*. Dublin: National Monument Service of Ireland (Unpublished. Available to view on request).

Waters, Ronan. 2022. "Piers, Harbours & Landing Places of Co Galway: Insights into the 2001 Report by Ryan Hanley for Galway County Council." Paper presented at the Harbourview Symposium, Documenting Maritime Cultural Heritage, Dublin, 26 April 2022.

Wilkins, N. P. 2017. *Humble Works for Humble People: A History of the Fishery Piers of County Galway and North Clare, 1800–1922*. Newbridge: Irish Academic Press.

3 Small-Scale Harbours
A Framework Approach to Site Assessment and Classification

Hilary Wyatt

Introduction

Given the enduring social and cultural importance of the UK and Irish coastline, the appropriate analysis and classification of the hundreds of extant historic harbours and landing places dotted along its length would appear to be central to assessing the significance and statutory designation of these complex heritage settings. However, both the National Inventory of Architectural Heritage (NIAH) in Ireland and the Royal Commission on the Ancient and Historical Monuments of Wales (RCAHMW) have identified significant inconsistencies in how built harbour-works and natural settings historically connected with maritime activity are designated within their records (Shotton and Prizeman 2022). Heritage records relating to the Scottish harbours have been strongly influenced by the surveys of the antiquarian Angus Graham and the gazetteer of industrial archaeologist John Hume, and their work is often the basis for statutory designation. Within the English context, although major ports are relatively well-recorded, minor ports, harbours and landing places are not understood at all and were identified as a research priority in 2014 by Historic England (Murphy 2014, 118). Jackson (2001, 3) argues that the smaller the 'port', the less we know about it, and to a large extent, this remains true.

Taxonomy and Classification in Heritage Management

The importance of taxonomy and classification within heritage management is well established, facilitating consistent site assessment, typological and comparative analysis, and providing a sound basis for statutory designation and the articulation of significance – often as a precursor to change-related decision-making. European Standard EN 16853:2017 (BSI 2017, 5–10), and in the UK, BS7913 (BSI 2013, 8) outline a best practice approach for the assessment of significance, which should include at a minimum, an assessment of the original design, the technology of its materials and construction, spatial character, how and why it has changed over time, any relationship to its wider

DOI: 10.4324/9781003385097-4

This chapter has been made available under a CC-BY-NC-ND license.

setting, and comparison with similar structures elsewhere. This presumes the existence of an agreed taxonomy, enabling the identification of similarities and differences within a professionally validated interpretive framework. However, no such taxonomy has emerged for heritage sites falling into the class of minor harbours and landing places.

This problem is long-standing; the investigation of early coastal settlements (Fox 2001; Heath 1968, 53–69; Kowaleski 2001, 2014) has been hindered by a lack of archival records relating to minor sites and the widespread use of generic terms such as *peer*, *key* and *getee* usually without further qualification. The same indiscriminate use of generic terms was identified by Vernon-Harcourt in his 1885 publication on harbours and docks. He contended that whilst it is sometimes difficult to distinguish between certain types of structure, such as jetties and breakwaters, they could be more usefully defined by the *purpose* for which they were engineered – their function rather than their construction. He also suggests the term *pier* should be reserved for landing places and promenades (Vernon-Harcourt 1885, 91).

Historic England acknowledges a late appreciation of the coastal zone (Historic England 2018, 1), and developed a new methodology – Historic Seascape Characterisation (HSC) as a means of producing a three-dimensional archaeological survey of the seabed, water column and surface (Murphy 2014, 12). In an explicit attempt to improve consistency within heritage records, the taxonomy employed by Historic England was subsequently collated into thesauri by the Forum on Information Standards in Heritage (FISH 2015). Although definitions are broadly function-led, only eight terms relate to harbour structures,[1] six relate to spatial characteristics,[2] and three relate to coastal defences.[3] In contrast, the FISH 'farmsteads' thesaurus contains 131 defined terms. Whilst the HSC methodology has enabled the inventorial recording of coastal heritage assets, it has not furthered the understanding of harbours as heritage *settings*. Furthermore, the use of such a limited taxonomy may have a flattening effect, obscuring functional differentiation between principal structures, spatial characteristics, environment, and settlement; and consequently, inhibiting an understanding of site morphology. This lack of technical definition is reflected in the inconsistent heritage designation of harbour sites, significant ambiguity in list descriptions and conservation area appraisals, and an almost complete lack of professional guidance (Wyatt and Prizeman 2018).

Research Approaches to Minor Harbours

A few historians have investigated the emergence of coastal settlements outside the port towns (Kowaleski 2001; Fox 2001; Lockhart 1980; Coull 1989), but their focus is the socio-economic development of settlements, rather than the harbours themselves. The British Fisheries Society (BFS) has attracted a disproportionate amount of research, given that only four harbours have resulted from its formation; however, research has centred on the architecture of the settlements (Maudlin 2007), their growth, and the operation of the organisation itself (Dunlop 1978; Munro 1989; Coull 1996, 2005). Although researchers acknowledge that in any new settlement, completion of the harbour-works was the primary factor affecting its eventual success, as yet, no critical evaluation of the harbours financed by the BFS or the Fishery Board – formed in 1809, has been undertaken. Fox (2001, 14) explicitly remarks on the lack of guidance to help the historian along.

> Were quays of different types? What was their chronology of development? Who built them? What relationship did they have with the settlement? At this stage we must be content with skirting around these questions.

Only a few researchers (Graham 1969; Graham and Gordon 1988; Johnson 2015; Hume 1976, 1977; Shotton 2016) have taken an archaeological or architectural approach towards the construction of harbour-works. Graham's scholarly examination of early archival sources is particularly effective in understanding the development of the medieval coastal Burghs, whilst Johnson's investigation into the 'timber sea-coast piers' of the English east coast examines the phenomenon of a lost class of structure which now survives only as archaeological fragments. However, the inherent risk in focusing on materiality and construction is that harbour-works are assessed through the familiar prism of land-based architecture, isolated from their function, physical environment, and use. As Stevenson (1874, 215) warns, "The requirements of marine masonry are, in many respects, nearly the opposite of those for land architecture." Furthermore, a perceived lack of architectural merit may well lead to under-designation; Graham goes further, arguing that the overall lack of architectural detail in harbour-works, together with the difficulty of dating masonry, prevents the classification of harbours 'in the manner of castles and churches' (1969, 206).

The lack of consistent taxonomy has led some researchers to develop their own definitions – for example, Johnson's 'timber sea-coast piers,' or to adopt the use of institutionally specific terminology. A striking example of this is the term *groyne wall* which was used interchangeably with *breakwater* within Irish Office of Public Works specifications and is retained by Shotton (2016, 2). Whilst Graham developed his own short taxonomy in his 1969 survey, some definitions lack clarity and are not consistently applied. For example, Cockenzie (Lothian) is assessed as having a west breakwater quay and an east breakwater; however, in Graham's classification of harbour-works, they are described as 'two converging piers'. His definition of a *jetty* appears to encompass landing stages, ferry slips, and the composite ramped structures typically found in the Scottish Highlands (see Rockfield case study below).

These variable approaches remind us that harbours are the complex product of supra-national, national, regional, and hyper-localised factors, which may be a significant challenge in establishing a single taxonomy that operates successfully across administrative and institutional boundaries.

Classification and the Influence of Civil Engineers

The adoption of Vernon-Harcourt's function-led approach is not without challenges; from the late eighteenth century onwards, the history of harbours became the history of marine civil engineering, a discrete discipline which developed very rapidly, undergoing a complete scale change in the early 20th century. Whilst the Proceedings of the Institution of Civil Engineers (ICE) enabled knowledge transfer from the Institution's formation in 1818, engineers themselves were working with incomplete knowledge of wave processes, and the lack of standardised engineering definitions and any analytical framework were barriers to progress (Allsop 2021, 135–139). Nevertheless, a number of early civil engineers involved in harbour improvement wrote prolifically, and these accounts are – with some extrapolation – a primary source in understanding general approaches to harbour design. However, it is important to note that as the science of harbour-works rapidly evolved, some terminology became obsolete, or was modified through subsequent developments in engineering. The term *breakwater* appears relatively modern and is used by Smeaton in his Reports (Smeaton 1837), but it is often conditioned by a supplementary term; for example, a proposed 'breakwater or bulwark' at Ramsgate (ibid., 222), and at Dover, 'a pier-jetty, or breakwater' (ibid., 233). The term 'entering vestibule' (ibid., 278) appears to have been later replaced by 'outer harbour' (Rennie 1854, Preface), whilst the term 'catch-pier', used by Smeaton in his Reports for St Helier (1837, 280) and Aberdeen (ibid., 169) also seems to have fallen out of current use. It is important to acknowledge that written reports tend to focus on large-scale works; for many minor harbour-works and vernacular structures, this type of explanatory account would simply not be available.

This brings us to the problem of scale. Whilst the concept of port hierarchy is well understood in socio-economic terms, its influence on the development of harbour infrastructure is less well understood. Large-scale port layouts could accommodate functionally discrete, principally built and spatial elements; harbour schemes of this size were well recorded, often reflecting contemporaneous innovation in dock construction and technology. A function-led taxonomy may be applied with some accuracy in these highly engineered settings. In contrast, usually due to lack of funds, the layout of smaller town ports may be comparatively incremental, evidencing the continuing use of traditional (and therefore proven) construction methods, the retention of technically obsolete structures (Johnson 2015, 336), or it may be the result of an improvement scheme only partly implemented as at Looe, Cornwall (Wyatt 2016, 105).

Outside the town ports, minor harbours may range from simple beach fisheries to industrial harbours built to serve a specific purpose. Typically occupying exposed sites and often highly constrained by want of funds or commercial volatility, their development may have required hyper-localised, sometimes resourceful solutions. In these settings, formal harbour structures (if any) may be multifunctional, with a greater reliance on the ad-hoc modification of natural features for shelter and enclosure. The relationship between environment, settlement and harbour is likely to be intimate and utilitarian, although not necessarily proximate.

In this context, the interpretation of a heritage setting through the application of a simple function-led taxonomy is unlikely to capture much of its informal quality, or its hyper-local characteristics, both of which are important aspects of significance. A framework approach to site analysis is therefore proposed as a means of providing a better methodology for the heritage recording of minor harbours and landing places. This approach embeds a clearly defined function-led taxonomy of structures within an analytical framework designed to capture the inter-relationship between formal and informal characteristics of a site, its setting, and the wider coastal environment. The case study below demonstrates its application to Rockfield, a small-scale harbour improved in the early nineteenth century.

Rockfield Pier – A Case Study

Rockfield was established as a planned fishing village in 1821 (Lockhart 2012, 256); it is situated on the Tarbat Peninsula, 3.5 miles from Tarbat Ness lighthouse to the north, and 1 mile from Portmahomack on the Dornoch Firth. Designed by James Mitchell, Rockfield Pier (Figure 3.1) was one of the first structures to be built by the Commissioners for the Herring Fishery (Scotland) for £430.00, with the landowner, James McKay of Rockfield, contributing a quarter of this (Commissioners 1830, 1–2).

A plan for a 'Boat Harbour and Landing Pier,' and a brief specification of works are contained in the Herring Fishery Report for 1828 (Figure 3.2). In the specification, Mitchell describes the structure as a 'protecting Pier or Wharf Wall' (ibid., 23). Its principal design features are the straight 2.4 m (8 ft) wide roadway – an 'inclined plane' extending circa 105m outwards from above the High-Water mark to a large rock near the channel entrance, and a NE facing 'protecting slope' specified at a batter of 2:1. At its toe, this slope is let into the reef at a shallow angle; it diminishes into the projecting bedrock from a point roughly two thirds along the structure's length (Figure 3.3). Mitchell's specification also proposes specific areas of rock-cutting, to level the bottom for the purpose of avoiding hull damage and creating a clear entrance channel along the Pier's inner wall by reducing the reef by as much as 2.1 m (7 ft).

Figure 3.1 Rockfield Pier. Reproduced with kind permission of Douglas Gordon, Trustee, Tarbat Discovery Centre.

Rockfield Pier is unlisted; the CANMORE site record[4] classifies it as a 'jetty' and cites Hume's description of it as 'early 19th century, A low coursed-rubble pier' (1977, 297). The CANMORE record also contains a brief descriptive extract from a 1998 CFA Coastal Assessment Survey and references Rockfield's entry in Graham and Gordon's survey of the north and west coasts (1988, 283–284). This summarises the Pier's financing and ownership, before focusing on materiality and dimensions. Graham observes the iron strapping to the roadway and the insertion of a slip to the head which is noted to be missing from Mitchell's plan (Figure 3.4). He also remarks on what is perceived to be a second departure from the plan, stating that Mitchell originally intended the 2.4 m roadway to narrow to 1.2 m approximately halfway down its length, although this is not explained further.

The village occupies a gently sloping ESE-facing site on a straight shoreline which is fully exposed to the prevailing north-easterlies. The shore is a steep shingle beach fronted by an extensive shore platform. Maximum tidal range is circa 4 m. The site is partly protected by Creag Charrach to the north, a long rock ledge which runs parallel to the Pier on an NW-SE axis. This offers partial shelter to the structure itself, relieving it of some lateral wave loads by forcing early wave breaking (Stevenson 1874, 13). The protective slope, also referred to by engineers as a *talus wall*, is intended to dissipate (and partly reflect) incident wave energy by directing run-up over the full surface of the slope – an attempt to reduce overtopping of the roadway and spilling into the harbour itself. The early nineteenth century saw civil engineers debating the use of sloping profiles as an alternative to the near-vertical breakwater profile

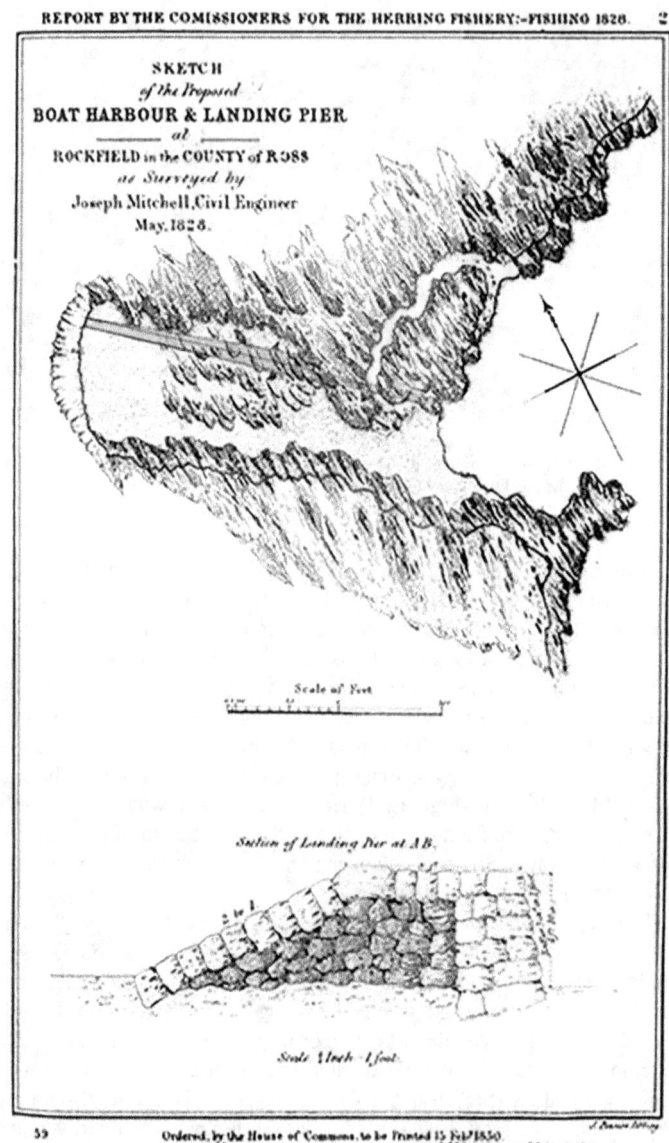

Figure 3.2 Mitchell's Sketch of the Boat Harbour & Landing Pier, Rockfield (Commissioners 1830, Plan 2).

Figure 3.3 Rockfield pier: protective slope. Photograph by Hilary Wyatt 2022.

Figure 3.4 Rockfield Pier: metal strapping to seaward end. Photograph by Hilary Wyatt 2022.

typically found in vernacular harbours (see, for example, Scott 1860). This clearly informed Mitchell's work implemented at Rockfield and at Sarclet.

From 1821 to 1829, Rockfield's 'harbour' comprised one or more natural or rock-cut channels providing direct sea access from the beach through the shore platform. However, these channels would only have been tenable during a very narrow half-tide window which would close on the rising tide at the point when incoming waves resumed their breaking over the reef, eventually submerging and obscuring the channel itself. Above the beach, a short slope leads to a flat area of ground once used for communal boat storage, curing and net drying. Whilst a later crab winch remains on site, it is likely that boats were hauled up manually.

Mitchell's structure is an extremely economical design which enables small boats to unload directly onto the roadway alongside, rather than on the beach. Its head dries only at exceptionally low Spring tides (Paterson 2023). The inclined plane allows landing to begin once there is sufficient depth of water at the head; as the tide rises, the landing point moves further up the inclined roadway towards the beach, and vice versa on the ebb. It is built in dry-jointed local Old Red Sandstone, minimising both material and transport costs. Apart from the angled copings to the protective slope, no special stonework is required. As this design is intended to be progressively submerged, extra costs relating to stair flights and parapets are eliminated – a row of light mooring rings is visible above the protective slope.

Whilst Mitchell's Pier was a significant betterment, it would not have eliminated the need to haul boats ashore. Provided the wind remained north of east, some shelter would be available in its lee, but this would be compromised by wave diffraction around the open head, and frequent overtopping due to its exposed position and low crest height (under 1.5 m at the midpoint). The small rock-cut basin to the south of the Pier may have been used for temporary moorings in fair weather, but without further enclosure, hauling ashore would remain a necessity. Rockfield remained a small boat harbour with an enhanced landing facility. In 1829 the proprietor was advertising the commercial advantages of the new 'harbour' to herring curers (Lockhart 2012, 192–194), and by 1881, the Herring Fishery Board returns state that 18 boats were working out of Rockfield.

Framework Analysis

Whilst Mitchell's structure is nominally a 'Pier,' its design incorporates both a protective slope intended to calm incident wave energy and a working deck on which catches could be unloaded; the inclined plane also facilitates low water access across the foreshore – these are principal functions associated with breakwaters, quays, and landing stages, respectively. Single, straight-ramped structures are characteristic of small-scale Highland harbours, but within this class of structure, there is considerable variation. An analysis based solely on materiality and appearance may invite comparison with nearby 'piers' such as Wilkhaven Pier, Easter Ross [unlisted] and Brough Pier, Caithness [unlisted], but these are institutionally built structures ancillary to nearby lighthouses.[5] Similar structures were built in 1848 at Applecross and Milton, Wester Ross as part of a programme of famine relief works, following the failure of the potato crop in 1846–47 (Goldthorpe and Dagg 2013 7). In fact, the only comparable structure on Scotland's east coast is Freswick Pier, Caithness (Figure 3.5), a more substantial work built in 1897 [unlisted]. Here, the later insertion of a concrete parapet provides a degree of additional protection from wave run-up and overtopping.

Figure 3.5 Freswick Pier, Caithness. Photograph by Hilary Wyatt 2022.

These examples confirm Vernon-Harcourt's view that the term 'pier' is too broad an appellation to be used with any precision; in fact, the use of generic terms may actually hinder typological or comparative analysis. There does not appear to be a definition in current use which describes the type of composite structure found at Rockfield. However, the term 'landing slip' has been clearly defined and employed historically. Mr William Lane-Joynt, giving evidence to the Select Committee on Harbour Accommodation defined a 'landing slip' as " . . . a place for landing from or going on board small boats, on the sea, estuaries, or rivers, running generally from high to low water of spring tide, which is gradually covered by the flood, and uncovered by the ebb tide . . ." (Select Committee 1883, 215).

More broadly, the lack of any established analytical framework is apparent in the existing heritage records relating to Rockfield Pier, none of which offer any analysis of Mitchell's design in terms of function and use. In the absence of this analysis, Mitchell's inclined plane is easily misinterpreted as a conventional slipway; the CFA 1998 Coastal Survey cited on CANMORE interprets the remedial strapping[6] as 'mounting points for boats or rails for keeping trailers on [the] pier'. As yet, Rockfield Pier has not attracted any statutory designation.

The Rockfield case study demonstrates the complexity of analysing, interpreting, and classifying a small-scale site. Its assessment has ranged from the modification of specific nearshore rocks to the early receipt of a small grant from the Fisheries Board, which in itself reflects national government policy requiring harbours to be largely self-sustaining. This assessment can be schematised into a provisional analytical model (Figure 3.6), which may offer a consistent baseline approach to data collection, site analysis and classification

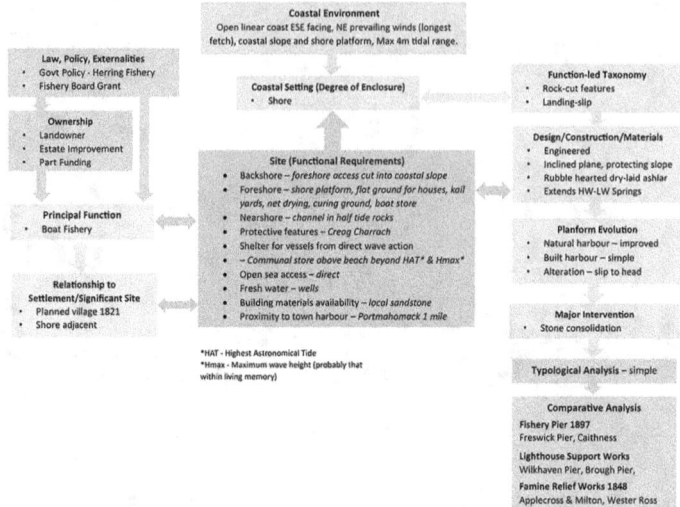

Figure 3.6 Framework Analysis for Rockfield – a provisional analytical model for the assessment of minor harbour sites (Wyatt 2022).

of small coastal sites, supported by a taxonomy, which should include natural, modified, and built structures.

Central to this analytical model is a set of idealised functional requirements, which are necessary for using any natural site as a harbour; once these requirements are satisfied, other key anthropogenic factors identified will modify the natural site and its setting. These factors are then sub-grouped, amended and tested against a number of sites to validate the model. Regional and national variations can be identified by applying the model to two or more culturally distinct study areas having coastlines with comparable physical characteristics, site uses, connectivity and levels of exposure. A key characteristic of minor coastal harbours is their marginality; significantly, this approach enables the qualitative assessment of sites that fall short of the benchmark functional requirements, by identifying how these shortcomings have been overcome.

Conclusion

This chapter has identified some challenges in establishing a single taxonomic classification for minor harbour sites. Whilst a function-led approach to the taxonomy of structures may be suitable for highly engineered sites or sites that have undergone several phases of development, it appears less suited to the granular heritage assessment of small-scale sites having fewer formal harbour structures and an almost ecological relationship with the physical environment. Equally, an approach which focuses on materiality and architectural style may have the effect of isolating harbour-works from their physical environment, setting and historic use.

Framework analysis is provisionally proposed both as a way of integrating the fragmented and somewhat impressionistic existing body of knowledge relating to minor harbours and as a means of providing an accessible methodology that orders and organises empirical site data to facilitate the systematic assessment and classification of coastal sites, their comparative analysis, and hierarchical differentiation. This approach also provides the baseline information required for assessing significance as outlined in EN 16853:2017 and BS7913:2013. This is an important step in ensuring that all decision-making related to these threatened and under-valued sites – whether in response to human-induced change or natural processes – proceeds on an informed and systematic basis.

Notes

1 Breakwater; jetty; quay; wharf; dry dock; wet dock; slipway and working pier.
2 Harbour pool; anchorage; creek; foreshore (three types); navigable channel (three types) and navigable river.
3 Seawall; groyne and sea defence.
4 Rockfield Pier, CANMORE ID15653 https://canmore.org.uk/site/15653/rockfield-pier Accessed 24 February, 2023.
5 Tarbat Ness lighthouse [Grade A: HES LB14100] and Dunnet Head lighthouse [Grade B: HES LB1890]. https://portal.historicenvironment.scot/ Accessed 1 March 20, 2023.
6 Storm repairs (rebuilding of the head and fitting 'iron lattice-work') were implemented by D & T Stevenson at a cost of £96 6/5 in 1851 (Commissioners 1852, 35). In 1881 a further £114 5/11 was expended (Commissioners 1881, 27). All costs were divided between the Fishery Board and the proprietor.

References

Allsop, N. W. H. 2021. "Old British Breakwaters: How Have Engineering Developments Influenced Their Survival?" PhD thesis, School of Engineering, University of Edinburgh.

BSI. 2013. *BS7913:2013 Guide to the Conservation of Historic Buildings*. London: British Standards Institute.

BSI. 2017. *EN 16853:2017 Conservation of Cultural Heritage – Conservation Process, Decision-making, Planning and Implementation*. London: British Standards Institute.

Commissioners for the British Fisheries. 1852. *Report by the Commissioners for the British Fisheries of their Proceedings in the Year Ended 5th January 1852; Being Fishing 1851*. London: HMSO.

Commissioners for the Herring Fishery: Scotland. 1830. *Report by the Commissioners for the Herring Fishery, of their Proceedings for the Year Ended 5th April 1829; Being Fishing 1828*. London: House of Commons.

Commissioners for the Herring Fishery: Scotland. 1881. *Report by the Commissioners for the Herring Fishery: Scotland of Their Proceedings in the Year Ended 31st December 1881, Being for Fishing 1881*. Edinburgh: HMSO.

Coull, J. R. 1989. "Fisherfolk and Fishing Settlements of the Grampian Region." In *Fermfolk & Fisherfolk*, edited by J. S. Smith, and D. Stevenson. Edinburgh: Mercat Press.

Coull, J. R. 1996. *The Sea Fisheries of Scotland: A Historical Geography*. Edinburgh: John Donald.

Coull, J. R. 2005. "The Settlements of the British Fisheries Society." *Landscapes* 6 (2): 82–95. https://doi.org/10.1179/lan.2005.6.2.82

Dunlop, J. 1978. *The British Fisheries Society 1786–1893*. Edinburgh: John Donald.

FISH – Forum on Information Standards in Heritage. 2015. *Historic Characterisation Thesaurus*. Accessed 24 February, 2023. www.heritage-standards.org.uk/

Fox, H. S. A. 2001. *The Evolution of the Fishing Village: Landscape and Society Along the South Devon Coast, 1086–1550*. Oxford: Leopard's Head Press.

Goldthorpe, N., and C. Dagg. 2013. "Applecross Bay Pier: Archaeological Evaluation October 12 to 20th 2013." *Highland Historic Environment Record SHG26532*. Accessed 24 February, 2023. https://her.highland.gov.uk/Source/SHG26532

Graham, A. 1969. "Archaeological Notes on Some Harbours in Eastern Scotland." *Proceedings of the Society of Antiquaries of Scotland* 101: 200–285.

Graham, A., and J. Gordon. 1988. "Old Harbours in Northern and Western Scotland." *Proceedings of the Society of Antiquaries of Scotland* 117: 265–352.

Heath, P. 1968. "North Sea Fishing in the Fifteenth Century: The Scarborough Fleet." *Northern History* 3 (1): 53–69. https://doi.org/10.1179/nhi.1968.3.1.53

Historic England. 2018. *Maritime and Naval: Scheduling Selection Guide*. Swindon: HE.

Hume, J. R. 1976. *The Industrial Archaeology of Scotland: The Lowlands and Borders*. Vol. 1. London: Batsford.

Hume, J. R. 1977. *The Industrial Archaeology of Scotland: The Highlands and Islands*. Vol. 2. London: Batsford.

Jackson, G. 2001. "The Significance of Unimportant Ports." *International Journal of Maritime History* 13 (2): 1–17. https://doi.org/10.1177/084387140101300202

Johnson, M. S. 2015. "Historic Timber-built Seacoast Piers of Eastern England: Technological, Environmental and Social Contexts." PhD Thesis, Archaeology Department, University of York. York

Kowaleski, M. 2001. *The Havener's Accounts of the Earldom and Duchy of Cornwall, 1287–1356*. Exeter: Dover and Cornwall Record Society.

Kowaleski, M. 2014. "Coastal Communities in Medieval Cornwall." In *The Maritime History of Cornwall*, edited by P. Payton, A. Kennerly, and H. Doe, 43–59. Exeter: University of Exeter Press.

Lockhart, D. G. 1980. "Scottish Village Plans: A Preliminary Analysis." *Scottish Geographical Magazine* 96 (3): 141–157. https://doi.org/10.1080/00369228008736468

Lockhart, D. G. 2012. *Scottish Planned Villages*. Edinburgh: Scottish History Society.

Maudlin, D. 2007. "Robert Mylne, Thomas Telford, and the Architecture of Improvement: The planned villages of the British Fisheries Society, 1786–1817." *Urban History* 34 (3): 453–480. www.jstor.org/stable/44614625

Munro, J. 1989. "Villages of the British Fisheries Society." In *Fermfolk and Fisherfolk*, edited by J. S. Smith, and D. Stevenson, 50–62. Edinburgh: Mercat Press.

Murphy, P. 2014. *England's Coastal Heritage*. 1st ed. Swindon: English Heritage.

Paterson, M. 2023. *Rockfield Pier*. E-mail to H Wyatt, 21 February, 2023.

Rennie, J. Sir. 1854. *The Theory, Formation, and Construction of British and Foreign Harbours*. London: J. Weale.

Scott, M. 1860. "On Breakwaters, Part II (Including Plate)." *Minutes of the Proceedings of the Institution of Civil Engineers* 19 (1860): 644–650. https://doi.org/10.1680/imotp.1860.23649

Select Committee. 1883. *Report from the Select Committee on Harbour Accommodation; Together with the Proceedings of the Committee, Minutes of Evidence and Appendix*. London: Hansard.

Shotton, E. 2016. "Technological Transformations at Boatstrand Harbour." In *Virtual Heritage Network Ireland Conference*, Cork, Ireland. https://doi.org/10.13140/RG.2.2.35882.62408

Shotton, E., and O. Prizeman. 2022. "Harbourview: An Irish-Welsh Networking Initiative." *Journal of European Landscapes* 3: 31–35. https://doi.org/10.5117/JEL.2022.3.87827

Smeaton, J. 1837. *Reports of the Late John Smeaton, F.R.S, Made on Various Occasions in the Course of his Employment as a Civil Engineer*. 2nd ed. Vol. 2. London: M. Taylor.

Stevenson, T. 1874. *The Design and Construction of Harbours: A Treatise on Maritime Engineering*. Edinburgh: A & C Black.

Vernon-Harcourt, L. F. 1885. *Harbours and Docks: Their Physical Features, History, Construction, Equipment and Maintenance with Statistics as to Their Commercial Development*. Oxford: Clarendon Press.

Wyatt, H. J. 2016. "An Introduction to Historic Marine Infrastructure in Exposed Tidal Harbours Construction, Plan Form, Materials and Repair in the Inter-Tidal Zone – with reference to the Winter storms of 2013/14." MSc diss., Welsh School of Architecture, Cardiff University.

Wyatt, H. J., and O. E. C. Prizeman. 2018. "Managing Historic Marine Infrastructure: A Conservators View." In *Conference Proceedings Coasts, Marine Structures and Breakwaters 2017*, 535–541. London: ICE Publishing.

4 The Role of National and Regional Bodies
The Historic Harbours of Wales

Julian Whitewright

Introduction

The coastline of Wales is studded with small coves, broad sandy beaches, sheltered inlets and extensive estuaries. These have been used since prehistory as anchorages, landing points, and places to beach all types of vessels for all purposes and activities. Over time, many of these locations have been developed and augmented, creating a diverse and striking collection of harbours: from the Dee Estuary in the north, via the rugged western coasts, to the Severn Estuary in the South.

The focus of this chapter is firmly on what can be termed 'small historic harbours'. These are not uniform in terms of their purpose, design, materials, geographic context, etc., but have evolved to fit the needs of the maritime cultures that have built, used, maintained, and in some cases, abandoned them. As their name suggests, they are generally small and historic, often occupying locations that have themselves been in use for hundreds of years, while being predominantly post-medieval or early modern in date. Their harbour infrastructure has often developed informally and organically over time to suit the people and vessels using an individual site. As such, in the context of Wales, the large, formally planned, comparatively uniform, industrial-era docks at places like Swansea, Barry, Cardiff and Newport, or monumental breakwaters such as those at Holyhead and Fishguard are not considered here.

This chapter begins by summarising the extent of Wales' small historic harbours, and related anchorages and landing places. This is followed by a brief account of the respective national and regional bodies that collate and maintain inventories of them within national and local registers. A short case study then demonstrates that in the 21st century, it is still possible to discover new harbour structures previously overlooked by heritage agencies. Looking to the future, the challenges posed by climate change to our historic harbours and our inventories of them, and the parallel opportunities afforded by advances in survey technology are highlighted. In doing this, the rationale for the need to update our holdings and records of these sites by national and regional bodies is addressed and set out.

DOI: 10.4324/9781003385097-5

This chapter has been made available under a CC-BY-NC-ND license.

Historic Harbours of Wales: Overview

As already noted, the historic harbours of Wales take various forms, in a range of contexts. A coastwise historical summary of many of these sites is provided by Jenkins (2006). Here, they can be summarised via a pan-Wales distribution map of the sites (Figure 4.1) and their respective quantities (Table 4.1).

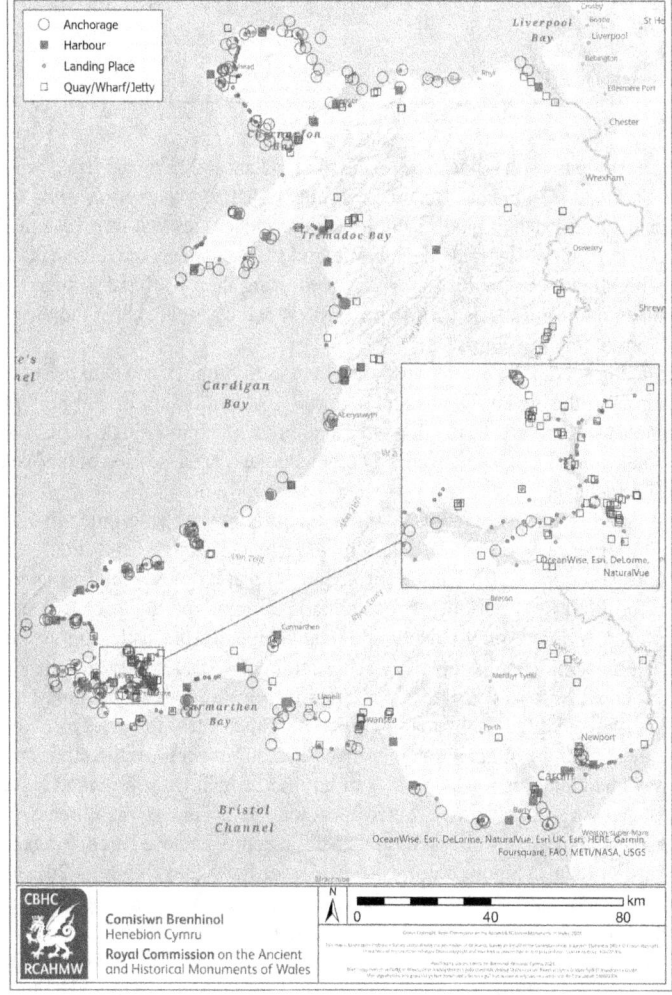

Figure 4.1 Overall distribution map of harbours and harbour-related entries within the National Monuments Record of Wales. Quantities of each site type given in Table 4.1. Map developed by Julian Whitewright 2023.

Table 4.1 Breakdown of harbour-related site types and quantities as held in the NMRW, distribution shown in Figure 4.1.

NMRW 'Site-type'	Number within NMRW
Anchorage	162
Landing Place	279
Harbour	49
Quay	95
Wharf	80
Jetty	11
Landing Stage/Pier	10

This encompasses the extent of the landing places and harbours listed within the National Monuments Record of Wales (NMRW), as well as sites with augmentations such as quays, and the related anchorages that were an equally crucial part of the rhythms of seaborne trade. Throughout, the representative sites highlighted in the text are referenced using their National Primary Record Number (NPRN) as used in the NMRW which is accessible via the Coflein portal (*coflein.gov.uk*).

Having set out the overall view, it is then useful to focus on a discreet area, in this case, the area of Dewisland in north-west Pembrokeshire, to highlight examples (Figure 4.2) of the diversity of approach within a single area. A pattern that would be repeated were any other similarly sized section of the Welsh coast be selected.

In some cases, geography is sufficient to allow the safe unloading and loading of ships within a sheltered inlet or cove. The significant tidal range around the entire Welsh coast permits the simple act of beaching near high tide, followed by a period for unloading/loading as the tide recedes before vessels are refloated on the rising tide. The village of Abercastle (Figure 4.2a) undertook significant export of agricultural produce and import of limestone in the late 19th and early 20th centuries largely through such a tide-based method with limited harbour infrastructure. Other sites, for example, Solva (Figure 4.2b), see augmentation of natural features through the addition of quay walls along one or both sides of an inlet, which itself provided a sheltered anchorage. By contrast, other inlets may be enhanced via a breakwater to provide increased shelter within the subsequently enclosed area, for example, at Porthclais (Figure 4.2c). Meanwhile, at Porthgain (Figure 4.2d), several approaches are combined, with breakwaters providing shelter, and quays facilitating the efficient use of the internal space of the harbour.

Harbours located in the lee of headlands, as at Porth Dinllaen (NPRN 403435), provide further examples of the opportunities provided for shelter by rocky coastlines. By extension, it is also important to highlight the similar diversity of approaches to utilising rivers for provisioning harbours. These can be at the mouths of smaller rivers, as at Aberaeron (NPRN 34169) or within

The Role of National and Regional Bodies   45

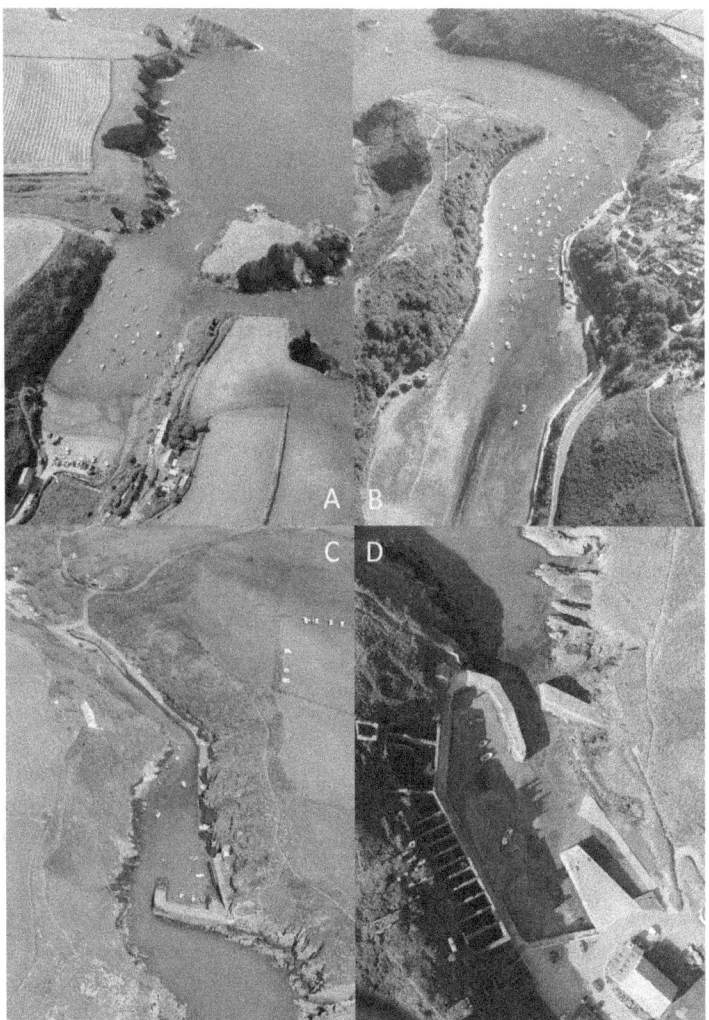

Figure 4.2 Four small historic harbours within the Dewisland area of north-west Pembrokeshire. From left to right: A: Abercastell/Abercastle (NPRN 268153). B: Solfach/Solva (NPRN 33210). C: Porthclais (NPRN 34342). D: Porthgain (NPRN 34343). All images © Crown copyright: RCAHMW.

the sheltered confines of larger estuarine systems, as at Porthmadog (NPRN 306317). Finally, mention should be made of those 'inland' harbours located on tidal rivers at a distance from the sea itself. Harbours such as Carmarthen (NPRN 34191) have their roots firmly in the medieval period and were still significant maritime hubs until relatively recently.

The above examples are certainly not exhaustive but nevertheless serve to make the point that there is no standard approach to harbour provision around the Welsh coast, even within a single area and a relatively homogenous section of coastline. Instead, we are reminded of the multitude of different factors that drive the selection of harbour location and application of a particular harbour technique or technology to an individual site. Such factors might include the underlying geographical context, available raw materials, size, nature and purpose of vessels using the harbour, intended function of the harbour itself, type of goods being imported/exported, extent of centralised control, etc. The result of this is to furnish the coastline of Wales with a richly diverse set of places and spaces that facilitated the interaction of land and sea in the past and which continue to do so, albeit in changed circumstances, today.

The Role of National and Regional Organisations Within Wales

The historic harbours of Wales, summarised in the previous section, fall under the remit of three different organisations from the perspective of recording their existence, location, general nature, and any legal protection. On a pan-Wales basis, the Royal Commission on the Ancient and Historical Monuments of Wales (RCAHMW) has responsibility for collating, maintaining and enhancing the National Monuments Record of Wales (NMRW). The remit of the RCAHMW covers Wales' terrestrial and marine areas, extending beyond the high-water mark as far as the edge of Wales' marine zone, and as such, records of harbours and related infrastructure are an important part of the NMRW. Crucially, this register is not restricted to monuments that are afforded legal protection through listing or scheduling; the NMRW is intended to record the totality of what is present, or in some cases, what was once present but is now gone. Of equal importance is that the RCAHMW has a remit to proactively conduct field surveys and undertake related research as a means to collect and collate new data on existing monuments. An example of a field survey is described in the following section, meanwhile, research and analysis of historic charts to identify historic anchorages and landing places and to incorporate them into the NMRW has been undertaken by the RCAHMW (Groom 2019). As a partner to the NMRW, the RCAHMW also maintains an extensive National Archive of material, for example, historic photos, relating to the sites contained within the NMRW itself.

Of course, the nature of many of the harbours within the NMRW dictates that they, or in some cases, elements of them, benefit from statutory protection as a listed building, a scheduled monument, or both in some cases. The decision of scheduling or listing a harbour or particular element of its structure is undertaken by Wales' heritage agency Cadw, which in turn has a responsibility to oversee the list of buildings, the schedule of monuments, and the statutory requirements relating to their protection, such as monitoring and inspection. All the datasets related to Cadw's work can be publicly accessed via their search portal (Cadw 2023).

At a regional level, Historic Environment Records (HERs) within Wales are maintained by the Welsh archaeological trusts on behalf of the Welsh Ministers in accordance with the Historic Environment (Wales) Act 2016 and are publicly available via Archwilio (2023). The HERs compile records and assign a Primary Record Number (PRN) relating to all aspects of the historic environment, including archaeological investigations. The records are an invaluable source for understanding the development of a site and any previous archaeological work undertaken. For example, broad-scale coastal monitoring projects undertaken in the 1990s (Sambrook and Williams 1996; Murphy and Allen 1997) are recorded as events in their own right (e.g., PRN 30751 and PRN 33470) and as events linked to the individual sites visited (e.g., PRN 24759) and recorded during such work.

Finally, the work of the National Trust (NT) bears highlighting due to the extensive holdings of coastline under their stewardship. As a landowner, the NT is ultimately responsible for the maintenance, upkeep, and ongoing preservation of the historic harbours on its land. The historic harbour of Porthclais in Pembrokeshire, having been in a derelict state, albeit still in use, for an extended period, was renovated in the 1970s under the oversight of the National Trust.

New Discoveries

The extent of the inventories just described, at national and regional scale, suggests relative completeness in coverage. But there is still scope for the fresh identification of notable historic harbour structures around our coastlines. One such site is the outer quay at Fishguard in Pembrokeshire (NPRN 704007). The site is not a new discovery, for it has never really been lost, rather forgotten about while lying in plain sight at the outer limits of Fishguard's old historic harbour of Lower Town. The stone quay is around 30m in length and 6m wide. It is formed with rough stone headers along its sides and end, and a rubble core. Although now much reduced in height and underwater at high tide, the quay is still highly coherent and a readily visible feature on the foreshore at low tide.

A routine review of RCAHMW aerial photos of the area during research for an adjacent terrestrial site led to the identification of the quay and initiated a field survey to confirm the nature of the remains apparently visible and to undertake their recording. This was successfully achieved during a single low spring-tide window, and an orthomosaic of the resulting dataset is shown in Figure 4.3. At the same time, recourse to the data held within the NMRW,

48 *Julian Whitewright*

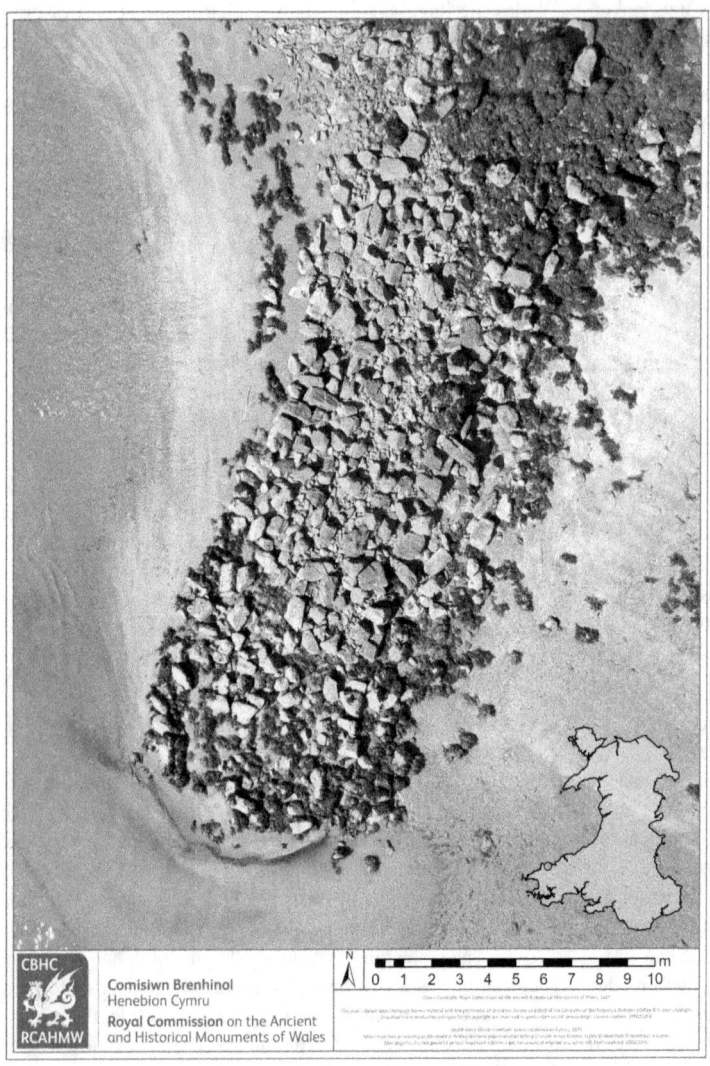

Figure 4.3 NPRN 704007, Fishguard outer quay. Orthomosaic derived from a drone-based photogrammetry survey undertaken by the RCAHMW on 19 April 2022 (© Crown copyright: RCAHMW).

by Cadw and within the HER indicated no existing monument or event recorded at the site. Parallel historical research focused on the charts of the Welsh coast published by Lewis Morris (1748) and held by the National Library of Wales. Morris' detailed coverage of harbours around the Welsh coast included Fishguard and clearly indicates the presence of a structure marked 'pier' in the same place as the newly identified stone quay. The convergence of archaeological and historical datasets allowed the presence of an outer quay at Lower Town to be confirmed, dating as a minimum to the decades immediately preceding Morris' publication in 1748. The field survey undertaken also confirmed the feasibility of rapidly collecting detailed 3D data of a piece of sizeable harbour infrastructure within the significant time constraints of a single spring-tide low-water working window. In this instance, the survey was undertaken with a small, sub-250g drone (a DJI Mini2). This technology has been rapidly adopted by the RCAHMW since 2021, alongside more established, larger drones, and provides an ideal combination of high-resolution results while also being highly portable. The latter is a critical factor for accessing many inter-tidal sites. The wider implications of this successful data collection for the longer-term approach to harbour-related holdings within the NMRW are considered in the next section.

Enhancing the Record

The current and future potential impact of the climate emergency on archaeological sites and monuments located in the coastal and inter-tidal zone is well documented (Harkin et al. 2020; Gregory et al. 2022), including within Wales (Barker et al. 2021). At the same time, this awareness has stimulated innovative projects such as the Wales-Ireland CHERISH project or the CITiZAN project in England, which are concerned with recording and documenting coastal heritage in the face of increasing coastal change, itself exacerbated by the climate emergency. The CHERISH project in particular, has highlighted the application of a range of existing techniques to a series of case study sites as a means to ensure that an individual site can be recorded and understood, not just in its own right, but in the context of a changing coastal environment both today and in the future (Barker and Corns 2023).

The natural extension of this work for a national body such as the RCAHMW is to undertake the proactive survey of coastal and inter-tidal sites such that the existing records, sketched out in the previous sections, are enhanced. This enhancement is not, in this case, through new discoveries allowing more records to be added, although there is always scope for more dots on the map. Instead, attention must turn to increasing the resolution of the view held within the NMRW to make the individual dots on the map more meaningful. In doing this, planning must be undertaken for a worst-case scenario resulting in a significant impact to, or even loss, of a historic asset such as a section of the harbour complex.

Envisaging such a scenario is not doom-mongering for the sake of it. Even within our existing records, there are accounts of buildings, sections of villages, and the like being lost to individual storm events in the past, as at Cwm-yr-Eglwys in 1859 (NPRN 304400). Meanwhile, recent erosion to Hurst Castle on the south coast of England has caused the catastrophic failure and collapse to one wing of the building.

Self-evidently, harbours find themselves at the forefront of similar potential impacts from increased storminess and sea-level rise, the impact of the former inevitably exacerbated by the latter. The records we should seek to hold for any given site should therefore aim to ensure at least a form of preservation by record in the event of major loss or damage. The best means to achieve this is through the suite of digital 3D survey methodologies now readily available and highlighted in a Welsh archaeological context by the CHERISH project. For historic harbours (in all their forms), this should mean a focus on the collection and collation of 3D digital data. This should form a baseline from which to monitor any future change (at a macro and micro scale) while also providing the best tools to interpret the harbour structures themselves, to inform repair in the event of loss or damage, and to facilitate wider public engagement through virtual access. An example of such work by the RCAHMW is shown in Figure 4.4, which illustrates the combined laser-scan and drone photogrammetry survey of the breakwater at Porthclais in Pembrokeshire. This survey was undertaken in four hours, during a low tide in February 2022.

Applying such methodologies may seem overly ambitious when seen across the entire corpus, not just harbours but of inter-tidal and coastal archaeological

Figure 4.4 NPRN 34342, Porthclais harbour. 3D model derived from a combined laser scan and drone-based photogrammetry survey undertaken by the RCAHMW on 20 February 2023 (© Crown copyright: RCAHMW).

sites within Wales. But projects such as CHERISH and CITiZAN, as well as RCAHMW survey work in the inter-tidal zone since 2021, have already served to illustrate how the application of technology can allow sites to be recorded with a high degree of accuracy and at a speed that would have been unimaginable a decade or so ago. At the heart of this survey agenda, however, must be effective communication between organisations at the national, regional, and local levels to ensure that effort and resources are not duplicated, and that survey results are shared effectively for reference by future generations. Finally, we must be reasonable in our expectations of the timescale when set against available human and financial resources and plan our record enhancement over the long term, to avoid disappointment that it has not been completed in the short term.

Conclusion

It is hoped that, despite the brevity of this chapter, the nature and extent of the historic harbours of Wales and the role of the various national and regional organisations in taking account of them is outlined in the preceding sections. More importantly, it is intended that the individuality of these anchorages, landing places, quays, and harbours is emphasised and accounted for. Such diversity of approach to the easily described routine of moving from land to sea and back again is what characterises these maritime places and spaces when viewed as an overall corpus of historic harbours.

The overall number of recorded sites and their geographical distribution within inventories such as the NMRW or regional HERs might give the impression that everything is accounted for. Yet as the example described earlier shows, there are new sites waiting to be identified, which in turn can allow for a better understanding of existing ones. Likewise, additional future analysis of material such as historical charts is likely to increase our spatial appreciation of these sites and their interaction with one another.

Finally, it is critical that organisations such as the RCAHMW continue to strive to enhance our records of these unique structures. Of equal importance must be that such work aims to create a digital baseline of these sites, using tools and methodologies now at our disposal. Such work will inevitably enhance our archaeological, architectural, and historical knowledge of such sites, as well as allow wider public appreciation and enjoyment of them. However, its primary aim should be to furnish us with a means to fully monitor, understand and take account of the impact upon them in the coming decades from the climate emergency.

Acknowledgements

The images are Crown copyright and are reproduced with the permission of the Royal Commission on the Ancient and Historical Monuments of Wales (RCAHMW), under delegated authority from The Keeper of Public Records.

References

Archwilio. 2023. https://archwilio.org.uk/wp/
Barker, L., J. Bullen, A. Davidson, J. Fairweather, and K. Laws. 2021. "Climate Change and the Historic Environment in Wales. Developing and Delivering a Sector Adaptation Plan." *The Historic Environment: Policy & Practice* 12 (3–4): 356–374.
Barker, L., and A. Corns, eds. 2023. *CHERISH: Sharing Our Practice. Investigating Heritage and Climate Change in Coastal and Maritime Environments. A Guide to the CHERISH Toolkit*. Aberystwyth: RCAHMW. https://doi.org/10.52405/RCW9781871184631
Cadw. 2023. https://cadw.gov.wales/advice-support/cof-cymru/search-cadw-records
Gregory, D., T. Dawson, D. Elkin, H. van Tilburg, C. Underwood, V. Richards, A. Viduka, K. Westley, J. Wright, and J. Hollesen. 2022. "Of Time and Tide: The Complex Impacts of Climate Change on Coastal and Underwater Cultural Heritage." *Antiquity* 96 (390): 1396–1411. https://doi.org/10.15184/aqy.2022.115
Groom, D. 2019. "Seascape Characterisation." In *Wales and the Sea. 10,000 Years of Welsh Maritime History*, edited by M. Redknap, S. Rees, and A. Aberg, 62–63. Talybont: Y Lolfa Cyf.
Harkin, D., M. Davies, E. Hyslop, H. Fluck, M. Wiggins, O. Merritt, L. Barker, M. Deery, R. McNeary, and K. Westley. 2020. "Impacts of Climate Change on Cultural Heritage." *Marine Climate Change Impacts Partnership Science Review* 2020: 616–641. www.mccip.org.uk/cultural-heritage
Jenkins, J. G. 2006. *Welsh Ships and Sailing Men*. Llanrwst: Gwasg Carreg Gwalch.
Morris, L. 1748. *Plans of Harbours, Bars, Bays and Roads in St. George's Channel* (Ref. AB 1043). Aberystwyth: National Library of Wales.
Murphy, K., and P. Allen. 1997. *Coastal Survey 1996–1997, Strumble Head to Ginst Point*. Llandeilo: Dyfed Archaeological Trust.
Sambrook, R. P., and G. Williams. 1996. *Cardigan Bay Coastal Survey*. Llandeilo: Dyfed Archaeological Trust.

Section 2
The Role of Communities

5 Recording Our Historic Harbours

Bill Hastings

Introduction

Each stage of the recording process has its own value and challenges: the making of the record, the storage and retrieval of the record, and the analysis of the record.

Techniques available include 'remote sensing' in the form of laser scanning, drone surveys, and photogrammetry; and more traditional techniques such as sketching, measured survey, record photography, and rectified photography. Survey methods that involve close observation of what is being recorded are particularly suited to community use. The record can be in the form of digital files or physical images and drawings on paper. New outputs such as photomosaics (Figure 5.1) and 3D photomodels, are readily accessible and are based on drone photography or hand-held photographs.

This chapter provides an overview of recording methods and outputs, their strengths and weaknesses, and their appropriateness to the needs of local communities. It is vital that we record our heritage, and it is important to understand that the survey record is itself a cultural artifact.

What Is the Purpose of Making a Record?

Making a record of a harbour can be for a variety of objectives, which include:

- Creating a record of the harbour at a particular point as a baseline against which changes can be observed.
- Creating a record that can be accessed remotely
- Analytical survey – the recording process as an analytical tool
- Engaging a community with their heritage
- Deepening our understanding of the past
- Understanding the role of the harbour as a climate modifier
- Learning from the past so as to inform planning for the future

Survey and recording methods vary in how they might contribute to these objectives.

Figure 5.1 Photomosaic plan of Sandycove Harbour, Dublin, assembled from drone images. Image reproduced with permission from Geomap.

Historic Context

Before embarking on making a record, it might be useful to consider some relevant matters.

Coastal harbours are part of our cultural landscape. They exist at points of connection between land and sea. Until the beginning of the 19th century, transport and travel on water was far easier than on land. With the coming of the railway age, that began to change. The Stockton and Darlington Line opened in northeast England on 27 September 1825, while in Ireland, the Dublin to Kingstown Railway opened on 17 December 1834 (Lewis 1837). But travel on water still held primacy, and the destination for both of these railways was a port.

Transport and travel on water go back millennia, and we know from the travels of the Vikings and Ireland's St Brendan the Navigator that distance was not an obstacle. Our ancestors travelled huge distances in small boats. They didn't use fossil fuels to power their craft, just muscle and the wind and sea provided the free highway to travel. No tarmac. It even provided food for the journey. Wooden and hide boats had little or no carbon footprint. There is still the potential for sea travel powered by wind. This travel may use sails or turbines or use hydrogen made from water through the use of wind-generated electricity. Coastal communities are well placed to exploit such renewable technologies. Hence, we should not value our harbours solely as historical artefacts, but as places that teach us how we once lived and how we might live again in harmony with the planet.

When surveying and recording a harbour, it is important to look for clues as to how the harbour emerged over time. Dalkey Island, a small island 200 metres offshore near Dublin in Ireland, has a very ancient history going back at least 6,000 years. Between the Island and the main shore is a 200-metre wide strip of water, Dalkey Sound, that was used as a safe anchorage by ships visiting Dublin for several hundred years (Gilligan 1988). These ships were serviced on the mainland by Coliemore Harbour, a natural harbour shown on old maps as a 'Landing Stone,' a large, natural granite slipway at the back of a small cove. There was no pier until the mid-19th century, and the 'Landing Stone' is still used by small boats.

Bulloch Harbour, a little to the west of Coliemore, is a somewhat larger natural harbour. In the 12th century, Cistercian monks established a fishery and built a castle there, which still stands. In the 18th and 19th centuries, Bulloch was used to ship granite across Dublin Bay to build quays and harbour walls and apparently parts of the Thames Embankment. Illustrations of the 18th and 19th centuries show that what are now public roads running along two sides of the harbour were originally quays. The main pier across the mouth of the harbour was completed in 1820 (Shotton 2019).

The history of Coliemore and Bulloch shows that the survey and recording of a harbour may unravel a complex past. Many harbours originated as a natural place of shelter, where a boat could be run ashore, or tied up so as not to be swept away in a storm. As boats became larger in size, piers were built in such places behind which a boat could take shelter.

Many smaller harbours have piers dating from the 18th and 19th centuries. These historic structures are now under threat by climate change, high tides, and increased storm forces, so there is a need to record them. But we should also act in a spirit of curiosity and optimism. Understanding the past can help us navigate the future. We not only need to protect our heritage but also learn from it.

Review of Survey Methods

When considering how to approach the survey and recording of a harbour and what methods to use, some methods may be more appropriate than others, depending on the circumstances. The commentaries provided below will be helpful in coming to a decision on what approach to take.

Direct Personal Observation of the Structure and Its Context

One of the oldest and most reliable recording methods is to make sketch drawings. While it is assumed that sketching requires artistic training, it is not necessarily so. The key is careful observation. By taking the time to observe what form or forms a structure is composed of, it is possible to make a sketch that breaks a structure down into its components. This is not a process of artistic creativity but a form of notetaking. If several members of a community are taking sketch notes and then collating and comparing them, then a very detailed understanding of the structure being recorded can be developed.

Freehand sketches can also be used to draw the context in which a structure stands. The context should be drawn in a simple outline. A sketch drawing should concentrate on the structure to be recorded. Sketching permits editing – omitting things that are not important, unlike photography, which takes in everything in front of the camera. Sketching must always be done on-site where the structure can be observed in the round. Sketching from photographs would defeat the advantage of seeing the object in three dimensions.

Direct measurement, such as with tapes or rules, means that those taking the measurements will engage directly with the details of the structure. Dimensions can be written down on carefully observed hand-drawn survey notes (Figure 5.2). Several people working together sketching, taking measurements and making survey notes guarantees community engagement.

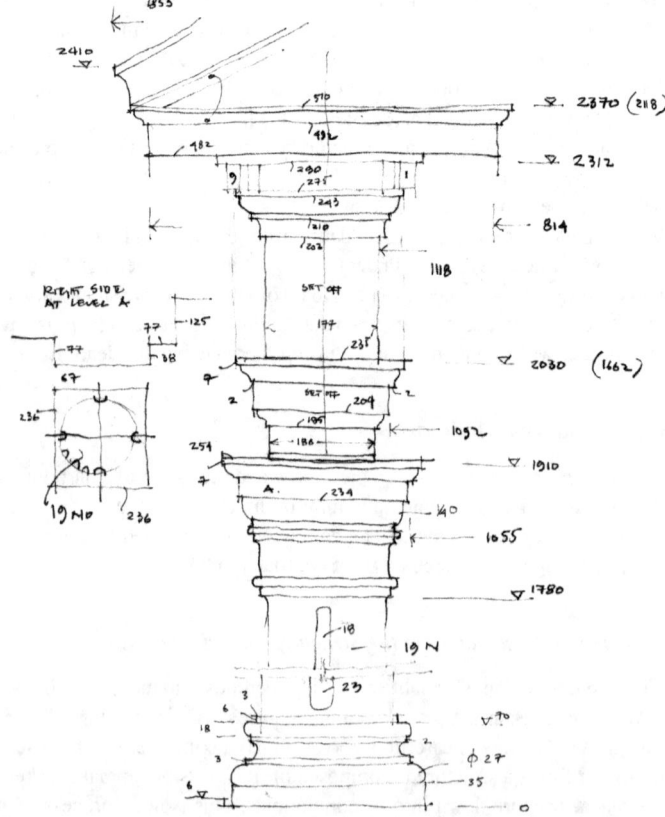

Figure 5.2 Freehand sketch of a building feature, with dimensions. Drawing by Bill Hastings.

Ideally, historical research should always be part of the survey and recording process. Studying old maps and images and old written descriptions will prompt questions that a site investigation might seek to answer. And the on-site examination of the structure might then prompt further historical research.

Traditional and Advanced Methods of Documentation

Traditional methods such as drawing, sketching, and tape measurement are ones with which everyone is likely to be familiar. The products of traditional methods, such as drawings on paper, are also familiar to everyone, and are unlikely to require interpretation or explanation.

Photography is a mechanical process with which, at one level, everyone is familiar and which produces a result that everyone understands. Photography can produce still images or videos and can be taken with a camera that is hand-held or steadied on a tripod, or with a camera flown on a drone. Taking useful record photographs requires care. Taking hand-held photographs offers the temptation to be casual about exactly where the camera is pointed or how the camera is tilted. The discipline of using a tripod leads to photographs being more deliberately composed.

The convention in architectural photography is that the camera should be level and not tilted back so that verticals in the structure remain vertical in the image (Figure 5.3). Taking flat-on photographs of the surface of a building or structure and at least two measurements on that surface allows the resultant image to be scaled, which is called rectified photography. Lenses used for record photography should not be too wide, no wider than a 24 mm lens on a 35 mm full-frame camera. Lenses with a narrow coverage, while useful for details, can omit relevant context.

Laser scanning is an automated method. The scanning instrument sends out pulsed laser beams in all directions, which reflect back to the instrument and create a virtual three-dimensional model of the object and its surroundings in what is called a point cloud, where every measurement is recorded as a point. Typically point clouds are very large digital files, and access to these files requires appropriate equipment and software.

Processing Data Off-Site

Off-site processing of photography can provide several useful types of records including rectified photography, photomosaics and photomodelling. Producing a rectified photographic image requires scaling a flat-on photograph. This is usually done in *Photoshop* on a computer, but other software can be used for scaling. Scaling a print can be done on a suitable photocopier.

A photomosaic plan or elevation can be made from drone photography composed of overlapping images (Figure 5.1). Photomosaics can be assembled off-site by post-processing sets of drone-acquired images using software such as *PIX 4D*.

Figure 5.3 Record photograph of the west face of St Begnet's Church, Dalkey Island, 9th century. This flat on image could be scaled to produce a rectified elevation. Photograph by Bill Hastings.

Recording Our Historic Harbours 61

If photographs of a structure have been taken from multiple different directions, these photographs can be combined to create a 3D digital photo model of the structure using software such as *Metashape,* or *Reality Capture* (Figure 5.4). Photomodels have a more photorealistic appearance than point clouds created by laser scanning technology because every point contains colour information from the photograph. These types of 3D digital models are more accessible in that even using a modest computer, the models can be saved as 3D PDF files that can be readily rotated or sliced into sections of the object.

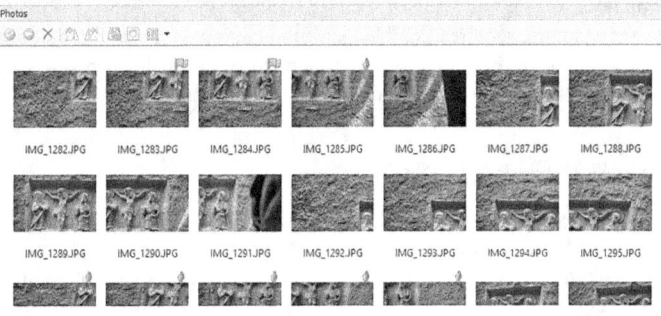

Figure 5.4 Photomodel of a carved wall panel, with some of the images from which the model was made. Image reproduced with permission from Ross McDermott.

Laser scanning requires processing to register point clouds acquired from different instrument locations with each other. Registering point clouds to each other may be done on- or off-site depending on the equipment and systems used. Extracting drawings from point clouds is usually done remotely by specialists and very often not by the individuals who went to the site. This can lead to serious errors, which is understandable if the drawing is being made solely by looking at a point cloud, and the person making the drawing has never seen the actual structure.

Level of Skill Required On-Site

Taking record photographs requires quite a degree of skill and judgement. Because almost everyone has a camera built into their mobile phone, people have become used to taking multiple photographs at the drop of a hat – and more of the hat after it has dropped. Taking a large number of indiscriminate photographs does not constitute a good record. The aim should be to gather the most information possible with the smallest number of photographs. This means that each photograph should contain only information that is relevant. You do not have to be a professional to take the right photographs, you just have to be observant and use photography sparingly.

Drone surveys can be carried out by amateurs to acquire photographs or videos. But to gather the overlapping photographs needed to create photomosaic plans and elevations (Figure 5.5), the drone has to be flown in controlled patterns both horizontally and vertically, requiring sophisticated drone technical skill to operate it. Tying the photomosaics to a national grid requires input from a professional surveyor using specialist equipment.

Photographs for photomodelling should be taken all around the structure, including from above. Care will be needed to ensure that all parts of the structure are photographed, each part from at least two directions. These photographs should be taken in flat light, as shadows may conceal important information.

Laser scanning requires knowledge of the equipment used and its operation. A scanned survey should be tied to a national grid using separately surveyed control points and measurements that will appear in the point cloud.

Level of Skill Required Off-Site

Record photographs usually need some off-site post-processing, particularly if they were taken with a handheld camera rather than one on a tripod. The photograph may need to be straightened, cropped to remove information that is not relevant, colour adjusted, or the shadows may need to be brightened. These are simple tasks for someone comfortable using software such as *Photoshop*, but there is a degree of skill required.

Figure 5.5 Elevation of a window of a church: Point cloud image to the left, Photomosaic image to the right. Image reproduced with permission from Geomap.

As we have seen earlier, making drawings from the point clouds generated by laser scanning requires a high level of skill. It also requires a high degree of skill and knowledge of appropriate software such as CAD (computer aided design) software or BIM (building information modelling) software.

Physical or Digital Records

Traditional records are physical: hand-drawn views of a structure on paper; survey notes in the form of carefully observed and freehand plans, sections and elevations; hardline physical drawings on a high-quality paper or drafting film; typed descriptions of the survey procedure; typed inventory of the structure and of its condition; references to historic sources; copies of historic maps; photographic negatives and prints.

Such physical records need to be catalogued and stored somewhere safe. Ideally, there should be at least two copies of the physical record. One copy might be stored with a Local Authority and a second in a library or archive. Experience has taught this author that Local Authorities or State Bodies do not regard storing records as a priority and that records provided to them are often discarded after some time has passed or simply lost or misfiled.

In Ireland, historic harbours are listed as Protected Structures under Section 51 of *The Planning and Development Act, 2000* (Oireachtas 2000, as amended), which also requires that Local Authorities keep records of these structures. All these Local Authorities publish lists of their protected structures, but the *Architectural Heritage Protection Guidelines for Planning Authorities* (DAHG 2011) for Ireland says that a more detailed file 'should contain copies of any descriptions, declarations, photographs, correspondence and maps' and 'should be kept in a safe store at the offices of the planning authority' (35). This implies that the record for each protected structure is expected to be both physical and digital.

The *Guidelines* also say in Section 16.1 that:

In the interest of protecting a historic structure, the development of a disaster plan can be useful, mitigating the endangerment of those parts of the structure which are saved from a fire, flood or other devastation. This could involve compiling an inventory of special architectural features and fixtures, a drawn record or photographs of the building or those parts of it considered as being of special interest.

Digital records are comparatively new. Thirty years ago, they were rare. Now, photography is almost entirely digital. Text is in digital formats. Point clouds are digital, and most survey drawings are digital. Digital files are increasingly large, and storage of large digital files is a challenge. Despite the increasing size of the files generated, digital photography is only now approaching the resolution of photographic negatives.

Photographic negatives and processing them costs money. Digital photographs cost very much less, which can lead to a tendency to take endless photographs. But, storing digital images does have costs and risks attached.

Digital storage media keeps changing. In the past it has included magnetic tape cassettes, reel to reel magnetic tape, various kinds of floppy disks, CDs, DVDs, Optical disks, hard drives, etc. None of these media are entirely stable, and much of the information stored on these media has been lost.

There are now new solid-state media and the Cloud. Will these be safe long into the future? Cloud storage has safety protocols where the same data is stored in several different locations at the same time and often in different jurisdictions. But the companies that provide cloud services make the rules, and you do not.

Given how much digital media has changed over recent years, with the resultant loss of data stored on obsolete digital media, it would seem foolish to expect that a digital photograph taken now would last well into the future and still exist in, say, 100 years' time. On the other hand, a print made now from the same digital photograph has a good chance of still existing in 100 years, particularly if printed on the right paper with the right ink.

Physical or Digital Access to the Record

It seems obvious from the discussion above that access to these records should be both physical and digital.

Physical methods such as sketching, taking manual survey notes, taking hand measurements, making physical drawings on paper, making on-site written inventories, etc., can all result in physical records, but these physical records are open to being digitised. Digital photographs and digital drawings can be printed. Still images of digital point clouds can also be printed. So having both physical and digital records can be achieved.

We have all come to expect that records of a place will be available online. We have come to expect that historic records and recent records can be examined and compared on our computer screens.

This leads to the question of interpretation. Every observer is entitled to their own perception of what they see. This in turn means that survey and recording should be objective and should not be seen as an opportunity to tell people what to think.

The European Landscape Convention (Council 2000) defines landscape as follows:

> Landscape means an area, as perceived by people, whose character is the result of the action and interaction of natural and/or human factors.

Our historic harbours fall comfortably within that definition. The phrase *'as perceived by people'* is central. Landscape, or Cultural Landscape is shaped by our observation of it. If our cultural landscape is only available on screen, our *'perception'* of it is blunted, and the landscape itself is undermined.

Harbours and the piers are real physical places. We should visit them and experience them in person, not just on a screen; smell the sea; and feel the wind. Harbours are part of our cultural heritage and our cultural landscape, and they also have a present life and offer possible futures. It would be wrong to see a harbour as simply a historical artefact, and so the survey record of a harbour should be open-ended and allow for future potential.

References

Council of Europe. 2000. *European Landscape Convention*. Revised 2008. Strasbourg: Council of Europe. https://rm.coe.int/european-landscape-convention-booktext-feb-2008-en/16802f80c6

DAHG. 2011. *Architectural Heritage Protection Guidelines for Planning Authorities*. Dublin: Department of Arts, Heritage and the Gaeltacht (DAHG). www.gov.ie/pdf/?file=https://assets.gov.ie/236448/369d5dcd-2194-498c-959b-eee826195011.pdf#page=ull

Gilligan, H. A. 1988. *A History of The Port of Dublin*. Dublin: Gill and Macmillan.

Lewis, S. 1837. *A Topographical Dictionary of Ireland*. London: S. Lewis & Co. www.libraryireland.com/topog/

Oireachtas. 2000. *The Planning and Development Act, 2000*. Dublin: Houses of the Oireachtas. www.irishstatutebook.ie/eli/2000/act/30/enacted/en/print.html

Shotton, E. 2019. "The Building of Bullock Harbour." *Cahiers d'histoire* XXXVII (1): 129–167.

6 The Role and Purpose of Digital Documentation for Marginal Heritage

Oriel Prizeman

Introduction

For coastal heritage, complex interrelations of concerns for conserving natural, built, and intangible heritage at a landscape scale overlap. There is a clear need to negotiate between compelling arguments for nature conservation, for enabling economic development, and for intangible and tangible heritage to coexist or to challenge one another. The rules are in flux, and hence, the arguments are more nuanced and perhaps less reliant on precedent than they might be.

The spectacular coastlines of South Wales have had a particularly fraught relationship with man that spans three centuries of industrial endeavour dominated by those founded on the extraction of fossil fuels and its use to generate heat for the production of steel. Parallels between Ireland and Wales were amplified in the Harbourview project, prompting future dialogue (Shotton and Prizeman 2022). Community workshops were used not only to collate memories and archives but also to participate in new digital recording techniques, sharing knowledge between international experts, local communities, academics and Heritage stakeholders (Figure 6.1).

The Harbourview project highlights the challenges of justifying the valorisation of marginal or infrastructural heritage. It raises new concerns regarding the ownership and custodial duty for that heritage. Who is responsible? What are the limits? How are the concerns of global and local governance to be balanced?

Draft ISPRS/CIPA guidelines to be presented to ICOMOS 2024 General Assembly identify six reasons for recording cultural heritage (Jan De Vos et al. 2023):

A) Assessing Values and Significance
B) Scientific Support for interventions
C) Creating a record in advance of destruction
D) Post-disaster recording
E) Intergenerational continuity
F) Educational value

Their relevance to the case of coastal heritage is discussed below, signposting challenges and future opportunities of digital documentation.

DOI: 10.4324/9781003385097-8

This chapter has been made available under a CC-BY-NC-ND license.

Figure 6.1 Harbourview History and Documentation workshop (above) and photogrammetry model of Newport quay generated from community workshop photos (below), involving Prof Luigi Barazzetti, Politecnico di Milano, members of local community, and representatives from the Royal Commission for Ancient and Historic Monuments Wales Newport Parrog, Pembrokeshire, Wales 4 February 2022. Photograph by Oriel Prizeman.

Assessing Values and Significance

Marginal Heritage

Marginal heritage is a term commonly used with reference to marginal communities, communities that are not recognised and therefore valorised within mainstream narratives of Cultural Heritage. Here, the definition refers to that of built heritage, which is not wholly conceived as belonging to a single domain. It also refers to built heritage that is infrastructural. The contemporary importance of cultivating a wider conception of the public domain to acknowledge such engineered connections has currency as an idea asserted by Easterling (2014) that is likely to expand future definitions of heritage.

Harbours are designed with the intent to secure the arrival of boats – to provide safe landing spaces, and shelter from storms and are universally conceived with the intention of doing this to the best ability that the economic and material resources that the time could provide. This emphasis on safety and utility over other design priorities such as aesthetic or formal planning schemes implies that they are engineered, that they are without superfluous complexities and are highly rational human efforts. However, their physical survival, often long after this instrumental purpose has waned, may yet precipitate a completely new layer of values to override them.

As economic imperatives change from harbours, say, actively supporting a thriving manufacturing industry to becoming primarily tourist destinations, questions arise as to the economic viability of maintaining harbour structures in the context of industrial inertia. By contrast, the historic fabric of the sites and the natural environment are both palpably threatened and increasingly at risk. Their aesthetic values, through proximity to nature and vulnerability to it, override the functional ones as exemplified in Mark Jenkin's 2019 film, *Bait*, in which a Cornish fishing village is overrun by second-homer urbanites for whom the economic value of the path to the sea serves a purpose of leisure as opposed to work, or in DeSilvey's account of the stammering management response to Cornwall's Mullion Cove in the face of Climate Change (2017).

Valorising Nature-Culture

> SINCE first the dominion of men was asserted over the ocean, three thrones, of mark beyond all others, have been set upon its sands: the thrones of Tyre, Venice, and England. Of the First of these great powers only the memory remains; of the Second, the ruin; the Third, which inherits their greatness, if it forget their example, may be led through prouder eminence to less pitied destruction.
>
> (Ruskin 1851)

Ruskin's statement exemplified the primacy of coastal heritage in human history and also illuminates its specific role in the documentation of disappearance. Considering Venice, he emphasised the essential requirement for the accuracy of drawn representation. ICOMOS has highlighted the Nature-Culture challenge in parallel with that of sustainability and climate change. Its 1996 charter relating to Underwater Cultural Heritage asserted the need for accessibility, non-destructive techniques and non-intrusive surveys (ICOMOS 1996); this statement foreshadowed the advancement of increasingly available digital tools in recent years.

The non-destructive documentation of both built and intangible heritage is a critical step in any process of evaluation or decision-making. The contribution of advancing digital technologies to this task in recent years has enabled not only a step change in emergency documentation but also diverse forms of engagement and participatory planning (Gregory 2015).

Many historic artefacts are incredibly difficult to measure and draw without a significant investment of time and highly skilled workers. The prohibitive cost of high-quality documentation would conventionally mean that for historic assets deemed low priority, comprehensive documentation would be avoided altogether. With the added challenges of submersion and disparate management responsibility highlighted elsewhere in this book, historic harbours have often been neglected. Today, however, as the workshops of the Harbourview project have demonstrated, accurate 3D digital models which record the condition, scale and form of such sites have been achieved using crowd-sourced imagery taken from camera phones and simple handheld cameras. The availability of low-cost drones significantly advances the capabilities of what would hitherto have been prohibitively expensive tasks to undertake using specially commissioned aircraft and boats.

Scientific Support to Interventions: Specific Challenges: Between Bathymetry and Topography

Bathymetry, the recording of the seabed, has a history going back 3000 years. Requirements for accuracy in support of navigation are obviously critical, and technological advances closely trace ongoing needs in commercial contexts, delivering ever-advancing kinetic systems to avoid the collision of vessels in congested spaces (Gold and Goralski 2012).

However, in parallel with the gulf highlighted by Wyatt regarding issues concerning the duty of care for the custodianship of harbours (Wyatt 2016), there is also a distinction between methods of digitally recording terrestrial and maritime assets. While the definitive edge of a harbour generates a legacy of discrepancies within record sets, this stems from both differing commissioning bodies and differing technological approaches responding to differing requirements. That said, there are emerging opportunities that may start to close this gap or at least make both more accessible.

For land-based data capture, the emergence of drones and the exponential facilitation of low-cost 3D data capture methods using photogrammetry have delivered a step change in capacity to record built heritage and topography in the last five years (Figure 6.2). As opposed to a reliance on manned aerial vehicles and more expensive laser scanning methods, inexpensive and accessible equipment and competitive software are bringing sufficiently accurate and detailed data capture into the scope of the most under-funded organisations.

The Role and Purpose of Digital Documentation for Marginal Heritage 71

Figure 6.2 Harbourview: Flying drone over Porthgain Harbour, resultant 3D digital model in Meshlab© and 3D print. Scanning, modelling and 3D printing by O. Prizeman, L. Barazzetti, and J. Gilchrist 2022.

For maritime data capture, expensive boat-mounted Echo-based or Light Detection systems have been advanced and may even be replaced with advances in Remote Sensing techniques using Satellite Derived Bathymetry and video data (Al Najar et al. 2022; Maillard 2020; Ashphaq, Srivastava, and Mitra 2021). Recent experiments in data capture of shallow water using Google aerial imagery (Li et al. 2021) and novel processing methods anticipate significantly lower-cost solutions to shoreline modelling. Airborne LiDAR Bathymetry has been successfully used to generate 3D data from an aerial platform in shallow water using green laser scanning where sonar systems would previously have been used (Wang et al. 2020). Marine robots have been used to collate underwater point clouds with photogrammetric models made from drone-captured data (Kapetanović et al. 2020). In addition, very recent work using machine learning and neural networks to model from images, as opposed to photogrammetry, suggests that traditional challenges of generating 3D data from reflective surfaces may soon be overcome (Belcore and Di Pietra 2022; Tonion et al. 2020).

Creating a Record in Advance of Destruction: Post-Disaster Recording

Digital Tools/Climate Change and Forecasting

In terms of understanding the risks to harbours, climate change research in Jamaica has underlined the urgency of seeking low-cost digital tools for modelling shoreline impacts (Acosta-Morel et al. 2021). Meanwhile, examples of modelling the impact of Tsunamis on harbours in Palma, Mallorca and Nice, France, illustrate the requirements for accuracy in such models, adding caution to acknowledge specific impacts that can be anticipated with more nuanced data (Vela et al. 2014; Labbé et al. 2012). Models can be used to anticipate future risks to coastal heritage (Anzidei et al. 2020; Westley et al. 2023).

Intergenerational Continuity: Digital Tools/Morphology

Historical datasets can provide a long view, which can be critical in forming strategic approaches. The beneficial characteristics of maritime heritage for supporting marine biodiversity have been mapped using a novel method of correlating data in a project in the Scilly Isles (Baxter, Coombes, and Viles 2022). Research in New York Harbour has highlighted the need to model long-term change (O'Neil et al. 2016). The non-destructive nature of digital modelling has also advanced the underwater archaeology of submerged ports and harbours (Georgiou et al. 2021; Diamanti et al. 2017; Diamanti and Vlachaki 2015).

The Role and Purpose of Digital Documentation for Marginal Heritage 73

Figure 6.3 Harbourview Storymap 2021–2 (Prizeman and Shotton 2022)

Educational Value: Digital Tools/Mapping and Engagement

Digital tools adopted for addressing built heritage defined as marginal generally commence with the adoption of GIS to map instances at scale (Calvagna et al. 2020; Elsayed 2020) or to create an inventory, as indeed the Harbourview project did. Figure 6.3 illustrates the GIS 'Storymap' generated for the project, which identifies the opposing historic harbours along the Welsh and Irish coasts.

In Sicily, 3D digital models have been created to allow diachronic engagement with specific fishing practices (Repola, Leidwanger, and Greene 2020). The potential for AR (Augmented reality) to support the interpretation of underwater archaeology is also being explored (Malliri et al. 2019).

With these new capabilities, the question evolves as to what the role and purpose of such documentation will become. Emergency recording scenarios apply continuously to Maritime Heritage. There are clear advantages to such accurate computable models to enable finite element analysis for interrogating structural repair strategies. The geometrical accuracy enables the potential for designing bespoke *in situ* repairs from the desktop, including, for example, 3D printed complex infill elements, which would previously have required complete deconstruction to design and damage to install. It is possible to map and quantify the extent of visible surface defects and so remove a degree of uncertainty from tight budgets, which have previously had to allow for significant unknowns. The higher levels of accuracy also enable better programming and organisation of work, which is so critically impacted by seasonal tides, to enable access for emergency repairs. Finally, in the event of catastrophic failure or collapse, an existent digital record can significantly enhance the potential for reconstruction.

Conclusion

Increasingly, the definition of heritage is expanded to encompass and valorise that not within the conventional canon. Industrial heritage and the heritage of Infrastructure leave new legacies which have demanded the development of new approaches and strategies for their care and management. Each step in this process is closely related to the issue of delivering suitable means of interpretation and also determining the extent to which access, either virtual or physical, is curated. Thus, both the valorisation and the curation of the artefact and the narrative surrounding it will force the conservator to adopt a position that requires justification.

Recognition of the significance of natural habitats and appreciation of the importance of their protection has increased in line with greater awareness of the vulnerability of our environment. In the context of climate change and of rapid technological advancements, the consciousness of the vulnerability of natural habitats is acute, and the hope for technological solutions remains prescient. Complex balances between socio-economic, environmental and cultural interests are all in play.

In the context of climate change, our most vulnerable built assets are those which directly face the sea. The preservation of historic harbour sites is thus at the vanguard of the climate change heritage challenge, just as Ruskin had placed Venice in such a position.

Beyond these services to the 'experts' who commission, manage and sustain such sites, there are further opportunities for more accessible and inclusive digital documentation tools to contribute to the augmentation of interpretation strategies for sites. The concluding symposium of the Harbourview project hosted at the Museum of Modern Literature in Dublin in 2022 drew together professionals, stakeholders, community groups and an interdisciplinary group of academics, validating the multi-dimensional engagement potential of the subject.

References

Acosta-Morel, Montserrat, Valerie Pietsch McNulty, Michael W. Beck, Natainia Lummen, and Steven R. Schill. 2021. "Shoreline Solutions: Guiding Efficient Data Selection for Coastal Risk Modeling and the Design of Adaptation Interventions." *Water* 13 (6): 875. https://doi.org/10.3390/w13060875

Al Najar, M., Y. El Bennioui, G. Thoumyre, R. Almar, E. W. J. Bergsma, R. Benshila, J. M. Delvit, and D. G. Wilson. 2022. "A Combined Color and Wave-Based Approach to Satellite Derived Bathymetry Using Deep Learning." *The International Archives of the Photogrammetry, Remote Sensing and Spatial Information Sciences* XLIII-B3-2022: 9–16.

Anzidei, Marco, Fawzi Doumaz, Antonio Vecchio, Enrico Serpelloni, Luca Pizzimenti, Riccardo Civico, Giovanni Martino, and Flavio Enei. 2020. "Sea Level Rise Scenario for 2100 A.D. in the Heritage Site of Pyrgi (Santa Severa, Italy)." *Journal of Marine Science and Engineering* 8 (2): 1–18. https://doi.org/10.3390/jmse8020064

Ashphaq, Mohammad, Pankaj K. Srivastava, and D. Mitra. 2021. "Review of Nearshore Satellite Derived Bathymetry: Classification and Account of Five Decades of Coastal Bathymetry Research." *Journal of Ocean Engineering and Science* 6 (4): 340–359. https://doi.org/10.1016/j.joes.2021.02.006

Baxter, Timothy, Martin Coombes, and Heather Viles. 2022. "Identifying Priorities for the Joint Conservation of Maritime Built Heritage and Marine Biodiversity: An Assessment of Shoreline Engineering on the Isles of Scilly, UK, Using Historical Datasets." *Ocean & Coastal Management* 227: 106288. https://doi.org/10.1016/j.ocecoaman.2022.106288

Belcore, E., and V. Di Pietra. 2022. "Laying the Foundation for an Artificial Neural Network for Photogrammetric Riverine Bathymetry." *The International Archives of the Photogrammetry, Remote Sensing and Spatial Information Sciences* XLVIII-4/W1-2022: 51–58.

Calvagna, Simona, Antonio Gagliano, Sebastiano Greco, Gianluca Rodonò, and Vincenzo Sapienza. 2020. "Innovative Multidisciplinary Methodology for the Analysis of Traditional Marginal Architecture." *Sustainability* 12 (4): 1285.

DeSilvey, Caitlin. 2017. "When Story Meets the Storm: Unsafe Harbour." in *Curated Decay: Heritage beyond Saving*, edited by Caitlin DeSilvey. Minneapolis: University of Minnesota Press.

Diamanti, E., E. Spondylis, F. Vlachaki, and E. Kolyva. 2017. "Surveying the Underwater Arcaeological Site of Cape Glaros at Pagasetikos Gulf." *The International Archives of the Photogrammetry, Remote Sensing and Spatial Information Sciences* XLII-2/W3: 243–250.

Diamanti, E., and F. Vlachaki. 2015. *3D Recording of Underwater Antiquities in the South Euboean Gulf*, 93–98. Gottingen: Copernicus GmbH.

Easterling, Keller. 2014. *Extrastatecraft: The Power of Infrastructure Space*. Brooklyn: Verso.

Elsayed, Doaa Salaheldin Ismail. 2020. "Reaccessing Marginalized Heritage Sites in Historic Cairo: A Cross-case Comparison." *Journal of Cultural Heritage Management and Sustainable Development* 10 (4): 375–397. https://doi.org/10.1108/JCHMSD-01-2019-0005

Georgiou, Nikos, et al. 2021. "A Multidisciplinary Approach for the Mapping, Automatic Detection and Morphometric Analysis of Ancient Submerged Coastal

Installations: The Case Study of the Ancient Aegina Harbour Complex." *Remote Sensing* 13: 4462.

Gold, C. M., and R. I. Goralski. 2012. "Kinetic Algorithms for Harbour Management." *The International Archives of the Photogrammetry, Remote Sensing and Spatial Information Sciences* I-2: 99–104.

Gregory, D. J. 2015. "Development of Tools and Techniques to Survey, Assess, Stabilise, Monitor and Preserve Underwater Archaeological Sites: SASMAP." *International Archives of the Photogrammetry, Remote Sensing and Spatial Information Sciences – ISPRS Archives* 40: 173–177.

ICOMOS. 1996. *The ICOMOS International Charter on the Protection and Management of Underwater Cultural Heritage*. Sofia, Bulgaria: ICOMOS.

Jan De Vos, P., A. Georgopoulos, P. Grussenmeyer, P. Haillot, P. Jouan, F. Rinaudo, M. Santana Quintero, L. Smith, S. Stylianidis, and A. Ya-Ning Yen. 2023. "(Draft) Principles for Recording Cultural Heritage." In *ISPRS/CIPA*, edited by ICOMOS (Unpublished).

Kapetanović, Nadir, Antonio Vasilijević, Đula Nađ, Krunoslav Zubčić, and Nikola Mišković. 2020. "Marine Robots Mapping the Present and the Past: Unraveling the Secrets of the Deep." *Remote Sensing* 12 (23): 1–39. https://doi.org/10.3390/rs12233902

Labbé, M., C. Donnadieu, C. Daubord, and H. Hébert. 2012. "Refined Numerical Modeling of the 1979 Tsunami in Nice (French Riviera): Comparison with Coastal Data." *Journal of Geophysical Research: Earth Surface*, 117. https://doi.org/10.1029/2011JF001964

Li, Jiwei, David E. Knapp, Mitchell Lyons, Chris Roelfsema, Stuart Phinn, Steven R. Schill, and Gregory P. Asner. 2021. "Automated Global Shallowwater Bathymetry Mapping Using Google Earth Engine." *Remote Sensing* 13 (8): 1469. https://doi.org/10.3390/rs13081469

Maillard, P. 2020. "Using Time Series of Sentinel-1 Images to Produce Dry Bathymetry of Rivers." *The International Archives of the Photogrammetry, Remote Sensing and Spatial Information Sciences* V-3-2020: 387–394.

Malliri, A., K. Siountri, E. Skondras, D. D. Vergados, and C. N. Anagostopoulos. 2019. "The Enhancement of Underwater Cultural Heritage Assets Using Augmented Reality (AR)." *ISPRS International Archives of the Photogrammetry, Remote Sensing and Spatial Information Sciences* XLII-2/W10: 119–125. https://doi.org/10.5194/isprs-archives-XLII-2-W10-119-2019

O'Neil, Judith M., Dylan Taillie, Brianne Walsh, William C. Dennison, Elisa K. Bone, David J. Reid, Robert Newton, David L. Strayer, Kate Boicourt, Lauren B. Birney, Sam Janis, Pete Malinowski, and Murray Fisher. 2016. "New York Harbor: Resilience in the Face of Four Centuries of Development." *Regional Studies in Marine Science* 8: 274–286. https://doi.org/10.1016/j.rsma.2016.06.004

Prizeman, O., and E. Shotton. 2022. "Storymap." *Harbourview*. www.historicharboursofirelandandwales.com/historic-harbours-story-map/

Repola, L., J. Leidwanger, and E. S. Greene. 2020. "Digital Models for the Analysis and Enhancement of Hybrid Spaces: Architecture of the Mattanza." *The International Archives of the Photogrammetry, Remote Sensing and Spatial Information Sciences* XLIV-M-1-2020: 443–450.

Ruskin, John. 1851–1853. *The Stones of Venice*. 3 Vols. London: Smith, Elder, and Co.

Shotton, E., and O Prizeman. 2022. "Harbourview: An Irish-Welsh Networking Initiative." *Journal of European Landscapes* 3: 31–35. https://doi.org/10.5117/JEL.2022.3.87827

Tonion, F., F. Pirotti, G. Faina, and D. Paltrinieri. 2020. "A Machine Learning Approach to Multispectral Satellite Derived Bathymetry." *The International Archives of the Photogrammetry, Remote Sensing and Spatial Information Sciences* V-3-2020: 565–570.

Vela, J., B. Pérez, M. González, L. Otero, M. Olabarrieta, M. Canals, and J. L. Casamor. 2014. "Tsunami Resonance in Palma Bay and Harbor, Majorca Island, as Induced by the 2003 Western Mediterranean Earthquake." *The Journal of Geology* 122 (2): 165–182.

Wang, Y., T. Kato, R. Abe, N. Maebashi, T. Tachi, and N. Kishimoto. 2020. "Accuracy of Measuring the Bottom of a Pond by Airborne Lidar Bathymetry (ALB)." *The International Archives of the Photogrammetry, Remote Sensing and Spatial Information Sciences* XLIII-B1-2020: 73–78.

Westley, Kieran, Julia Nikolaus, Ahmad Emrage, Nic Flemming, and Andrew Cooper. 2023. "The Impact of Coastal Erosion on the Archaeology of the Cyrenaican Coast of Eastern Libya." *PLoS One* 18: e0283703-e03.

Wyatt, Hilary. 2016. "An Introduction to Historic Marine Infrastructure in Exposed Tidal Harbours Construction, Plan Form, Materials and Repair in the Inter-Tidal Zone with Reference to the Storms of Winter 2013/2014." Cardiff University MSc Sustainable Building Conservation dissertation. (unpublished)

7 Ballydehob Quay and Its Small Satellite Quays

Cormac Levis

Geographical and Historical Context

The village of Ballydehob nestles snugly into the side of a hill at the start of the Mizen Peninsula in south-west Cork. A few hundred yards to the southeast of the village, the Quay, with its terrace of old stores and dwelling houses, is situated on the upper reaches of a long, narrow, shallow inlet off Roaringwater Bay (Figure 7.1). As the tide nears low water, a narrow, shallow channel is revealed, winding its way down through the slob banks to the much wider and deeper waters of the outer harbour, about half a mile from the Quay. At high water, boats of 50 tons or more can navigate right to the Quay.

Now long abandoned as commercial thoroughfares, small inshore creeks like Ballydehob once played a vital role in the economies of local communities when waterborne transport was the only means of conveying bulk quantities of raw materials, commercial supplies and agricultural produce. Although a definite date for the construction of the Quay and its buildings has yet to be determined, they were most likely built by a member of the Swanton family in the 1760s. Around the same time, another branch of the family built stores and a boathouse on the east side of the narrow channel, directly opposite the Quay (Ballydehob 1994). The structures on both sites were of locally quarried siltstone and sandstone.

Both the stores on the Quay and the eastern stores acted as granaries, facilitating the export of corn and as warehouses for incoming commercial supplies. Pre-famine, copper and lead ores, from mines just to the north of the village, were exported directly to Swansea, and limestone was imported for a commercial limekiln, which was located near the Quay. In the 1830s and early 1840s, timber was imported from New Brunswick, the timber ships returning to Canada with emigrants (Ballydehob 1994; Courtenay 1845, 959). These coffin ships continued to ply their trade from Ballydehob right through the Famine (O'Malley 1999, 21). In 1846, James H. Swanton, the proprietor of the stores, imported a cargo of wheat for the starving of Ballydehob (Hickey 2002, 154). The following year, two further cargos of food were discharged at the Quay, courtesy of the British Relief Association (Hickey 2002, 179, 191).

DOI: 10.4324/9781003385097-9

This chapter has been made available under a CC-BY-NC-ND license.

Figure 7.1 An aerial view of Ballydehob, 22/10/1982, courtesy of Irish Examiner Archives (Richard Mills). Ballydehob, on the northern extremity of Roaringwater Bay, was ideally positioned as a commercial gateway to the interior at a time when trade was largely waterborne. The Quay, in the centre of the photo, is located a few hundred meters south-east of the hillside village.

The eastern stores (Figure 7.2) fell into disuse around 1875. They were exploited as a source of building stone over the next 60 years and gradually demolished (Ballydehob 1994). From 1889, the stores on the Quay were used for coal. At this time, a large fleet of sailing craft, mainly schooners and ketches, traded cross-channel between Britain and the east and south coasts of Ireland. Varying from as little as 60 to 250 tons burden, they were a common sight in creeks and small harbours along the coast. It was these vessels that brought coal from Merseyside and Newport in Gwent to Ballydehob (Levis 1996, 119–124).

The coastal towns and villages of West Cork had long been supplied with commercial provisions from Cork by coastal trading vessels. Sailing boats of

Figure 7.2 Row of houses along the pier at Ballydehob, Co. Cork, c. 1920 (Fergus O'Connor Collection, OCO 163, courtesy of the National Library of Ireland). The two boats were part of a local fleet of sand dredgers that supplied the farming community with lime-rich sea sand to fertilise the acid soil of West Cork. By this time, the warehouse was used as a store for coal imported from England and Wales.

40 to 60 feet in length, they faced stiff opposition from the railways as the network expanded westwards. They came into their own again, however, in the early 1920s, when road and rail connections were constantly disrupted during the Irish War of Independence and the ensuing Civil War. In those days, one of these boats would arrive at Ballydehob Quay once a week with supplies for the many businesses in the village. Horses and carts would draw up on the quay to deliver the goods to the shops and pubs and return with butter, crates of eggs, and empty barrels for the return trip to Cork. By this time, many of them had been fitted with auxiliary engines, enabling them to compete very successfully with the railways up to the early 1930s (Levis 1996, 119–124).

Boats from the many islands in Roaringwater Bay accounted for much of the traffic in the Harbour. Ballydehob was the main market village for many islanders, and on the market day, a long line of small two-oar and four-oar boats would make their way up the channel, lug sails set if the wind was favourable. Some would have eggs, butter, and fish to sell. Some would have wrack timber to be cut into planks or corn to be milled. Others would have a plough or other farm implements to be repaired. Having tied up at the quay, the women would make their way into the village carrying their baskets of eggs on their heads. Having sold their eggs and butter, they went shopping while the men would arrange for milling to be done or do business with a blacksmith or carpenter. On the day of a cattle fair, larger boats would arrive with cattle and early in summer, pigs would be bought at the pig fair and carried home in bags. Tables, chairs, dressers, settles, beds, clothes, shoes, donkey and horse carts and harnesses, coffins, church pews, oars, boats and anchors, all made in Ballydehob, found their way back down to the islands. Coal could be conveniently bought on the quay or a boatload of turf from farmers.

Historically, Ballydehob Quay was usually referred to as 'the sand quay'. The provision of sea sand for use as an agricultural fertiliser was once a big industry on some parts of the coast, particularly so in West Cork. It has a history stretching back over 700 years, but it was at its peak, as one might expect, just before the Famine. With the cessation of marginal land reclamation and the declining population in the wake of the Famine, together with the availability of new fertilisers like guano, crushed bone and nitrates, there was a steady decline in sanding (Levis 1997, 108). By the 1920s there were only two or three commercial, eight-ton sand boats landing sand regularly at Ballydehob Quay (Figure 7.2).

With the scarcity of artificial fertilisers during the years of the Second World War, however, there was a huge demand for sea sand again, and no fewer than nine boats were soon landing sand at Ballydehob once more (Levis 2008, 292). This was one of the busiest periods in the history of the Quay. The sand boats, driven by sail and oar, dredged sand out in Roaringwater Bay and landed at the Quay on every tide, night and day. The farmers, carting the sand inland, were unable to keep up with the constant supply, so mounds of sand would build up all along the edge of the Quay and the adjacent road. Even then, it continued, the boatmen shovelling the sand back towards the centre of the Quay to make room for more. The islanders also cashed in on the bonanza, landing kelp and seaweed, which was just as eagerly sought after.

Most farmers lucky enough to have land extending to the foreshore were boat owners, either individually or in partnerships. As well as harvesting seaweed on the shore and on off-shore rocks, many of them dredged the seabed for a species of light, wool-like seaweed known locally by the Irish term *Leoithín* (Levis 1996, 112), and many of them had small private quays of their own. There were also larger quays servicing an entire townland. Between Ballydehob Quay and the open waters of Roaringwater Bay, there are a total of 14 of these small quays, all within two and a half miles of Ballydehob. Most were built in the second half of the nineteenth century.

While sand remained an important alternative to artificial fertilisers after the Second World War, it now came from a different source. While two boats continued to land at Ballydehob up to 1959, they could not compete with lorries hauling sand from the sand dunes in Barley Cove directly to the farmyard. Improved road transport had already put an end to the coastal traders, the last one calling in 1932 (Ballydehob 1994). Coal was now also delivered to the village by lorry, and the days of the schooners were over. With a dwindling island population and the eventual demise of the Ballydehob fair, boats from the islands seldom tied up at the Quay. Ballydehob Harbour became a quickly fading memory.

The Project

Considering, then, the obvious historical, cultural, social, and indeed architectural significance of the surviving infrastructure of Ballydehob Harbour, its omission from Ireland's National Inventory of Architectural Heritage (NIAH) and the local Architectural Conservation Area is both surprising and disappointing. Neither is it included in Cork County Council's record of protected structures. In light of these glaring oversights, the Harbourview project took on a particular significance for our team of community volunteers and, as we set out to document our local maritime heritage, we were mindful not only of the risk posed to it by climate change but also by societal apathy, by neglect of maintenance, and by both past and potential careless interference with elements of the infrastructure.

Having received instruction on 3D digital recording and visualisation techniques from Dr Elizabeth Shotton and ARC Architectural Consultants, our multi-skilled group of 13 volunteers set out to document Ballydehob Quay and its small satellite quays. It was envisaged that a 3D *Agisoft Metashape* model of the Quay and its buildings, based on a drone survey, would be a central element of our documentation. Tom Vaughan, a professional drone pilot with many years of experience, proceeded to undertake no fewer than three surveys. While the first two surveys captured the overall, aesthetically pleasing quality of the architecture perfectly, along with the stunning natural beauty of the immediate area, their primary value for the purposes of our project was in illustrating the subtle effects of light and shadow and range on the definition of detail that was vital for the purposes of documentation. With a greater emphasis on this aspect of the recording, Tom undertook a third survey, which was duly converted into a very successful 3D model by our Agisoft expert, Julianna O'Donoghue (Figure 7.3).

The production of scale-accurate elevations was our next consideration. While these could easily be generated from a drone survey, Sarah Canty volunteered to try her hand at ground-level rectified photography. She was aided by Anke Eckardt, while Julianna O'Donoghue again carried out the Agisoft processing. The photographers encountered considerable difficulty in keeping the image plane in the camera parallel to the surfaces being recorded. This delayed the entire procedure, leading to a prolonged time lapse between photos, which was an issue due to the changing profile of the quay wall with the ebbing tide (Figure 7.4). While the resulting elevation had, as expected, very obvious flaws, it was clearly evident that the difficulties encountered by the

Figure 7.3 An image of the 3D model of Ballydehob Quay and its buildings, which was generated by Julianna O'Donoghue, using the Agisoft Programme, from a drone survey undertaken by Tom Vaughan in 2021.

Figure 7.4 A series of rectified photos taken by Sarah Canty, helped by Anke Eckardt, used to produce an elevation of the Quay and buildings in 2021.

photographers could be easily obviated by a little more practice and, ideally, the procurement of a camera with integral level, plumb and rotation indicators (Figure 7.5). Another factor to be considered in ground-level photography, of course, is the terrain and its suitability as a platform from which to work. In our case, the seaward side of the structure could not be photographed at the required range because, although the area dries out fully with the ebbing tide, the foreshore consists of a deep bank of mud which cannot be traversed. The advantages of using drone photography to produce scale-accurate elevations are obvious.

Figure 7.5 Composite elevation of former warehouse building on Quay from rectified photographs by Canty and Eckardt 2021, with modelling by Julianna O'Donoghue 2022.

Figure 7.6 A detail of the Quay wall showing pinnings and traces of lime mortar. Photograph by Kevin O'Farrell 2021.

While photogrammetry is undisputedly an indispensable tool in the technical documentation of physical structures, conventional photography comes into its own in highlighting details that, although visible, may become part of the wallpaper in the wider focus of photogrammetry views. The subjective nature of conventional photography can also easily address issues around the effects of human interference or neglect on the site. In our case, Kevin O'Farrell's photographic survey proved invaluable in this regard.

Among the construction details brought to light in Kevin's photographs was the use of fine sea gravel and lime mortar in the quay wall (Figure 7.6). After two and a half centuries of tides ebbing and flowing, most of the mortar has been washed away so that, to the casual observer today, the quay appears to be of dry stone construction. Also of note is the use of thousands of small stones wedged between the larger ones. Known as 'pinnings' (McAfee 2009)

Figure 7.7 The original pitch line of the roof of the warehouse and the outline of the crane door can be discerned. Photograph by Kevin O'Farrell 2021.

by stonemasons, their function was to reduce the width of the mortar joint and to keep the larger stones in place until the mortar cured. A photo of the gable of what was once the old warehouse, now a dwelling, reveals signs of an alteration to the pitch of the roof and the location of the crane door that once opened off the first floor (Figure 7.7).

The neglected state of the quay is very evident in Kevin's photos, with large potholes in the deck and the flight of steps leading down to the edge of the low-water channel at the east end, in a crumbling condition. The most serious structural damage, however, was caused by the installation of a sewer pipe in the 1980s, when Cork County Council excavated a deep trench through the north wall of the quay, across the deck and through the south wall. The damage to the walls was repaired in a most unprofessional manner, with many stones haphazardly placed and no attempt made to re-cap the walls evenly. A stone bollard was dug up and discarded; the author replaced it with a similar stone in later years. All this destruction, along with minor irritants, such as inappropriate signage, are recorded in Kevin's survey.

As of yet, Ballydehob's small satellite quays, referred to above, remain largely unrecorded due to the pressures of time on the part of our volunteers. However, the drastically deteriorated state of the tiny private quays is evidenced by a preliminary photographic survey carried out by Dr Shotton, assisted by Julia Barrett and the author. The condition of the larger townland quays varies from very good to neglected and in need of repair. The

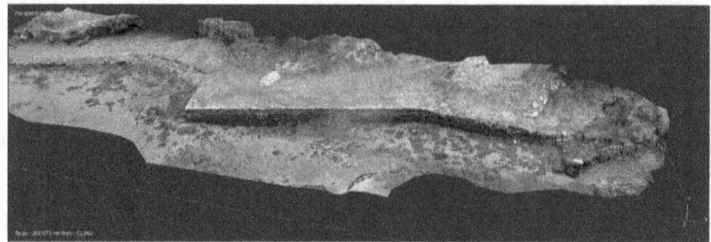

Figure 7.8 An image of the 3D model of Greenmount Quay. Drone photography and computer modelling by Julianna O'Donoghue 2021.

survey also illustrates the poor quality of the dry stone construction in the private quays relative to the professionally built, mortar-bedded stonework of the townland quays. One of the latter was encased in concrete at one stage, possibly during the 1930s or 1940s when Cork County Council's Committee of Agriculture actively promoted the procurement of sea sand. Another is possibly entirely constructed of concrete, replacing an earlier stone quay (of different configuration) recorded in the late nineteenth-century Ordnance Survey. Again, this was probably built by Cork County Council in the 1930s or 1940s. Many of the smaller quays were simply rock outcrops faced with stone and levelled off with small field stones or beach stones and decked along the edges, at least to some extent, with relatively flat flags. Further to Dr Shotton's survey, a drone survey and 3D digital model of Greenmount Quay (Figure 7.8) executed by Julianna O'Donoghue, further illustrates the good build quality of the townland quays.

A Range of Approaches and Inputs

With a cornucopia of skills and talents to draw upon and a wide range of interests, some of our volunteers pursued a more artistic approach to documentation. Writer and artist Brian Lalor, whose main focus is on topography, prepared preliminary sketches for a series of illustrations depicting the evolving landscape in the harbour area over a period of time ranging from pre-development down to the present day. Anke Eckhardt, boatbuilder, artist and model maker, designed and illustrated a paper model kit of the Quay and its buildings to take its place in her 'TinyIreland' collection, which is widely available in craft shops and other outlets.

Eugene McSweeney, local historian and organiser of heritage events and lectures expanded the scope of the project to cover other structures of equally significant heritage value in the vicinity of the Quay. He has written three articles for publication in a local historical journal. Finola Finlay and Robert Harris, well known for their blog *Roaringwater Journal*, where they publish on a wide range of disciplines, including history and archaeology, have focused on the neighbouring harbour of Rossbrin. Eoin Fannon, a practising barrister and a contributor to *The Atlas Of The Irish Coast* and to conferences on the law of the sea, provided expert knowledge on a wide range of governmental, administration and jurisprudence issues pertaining to the maritime environment and coastal infrastructure. Denis O'Brien, a quantity surveyor whose ancestors were heavily involved in the building of many of our historic structures locally, imparted a valuable understanding of construction techniques and specifications. Anne-Marie Birken, the current owner and resident of the buildings on the Quay, facilitated numerous photographic and drone surveys of her home. As a solicitor, her interpretation of title deeds and conveyances was extremely useful in tracing the occupancy history of the buildings. As chairman of the local Tidy Towns Committee, John Forde actively promotes public interest in our built heritage. His advice, encouragement, and support were highly valued. The role of the author, a local maritime historian, was to provide historical context and coordinate the efforts of the team overall.

Conclusion and Recommendations

The series of drone surveys, 3D digital models, photogrammetry elevations, photographic surveys, essays, craft work and artwork produced by our team, while requiring further refinement, is ample evidence of the potential capacity of local communities in successfully recording and documenting their endangered maritime infrastructure and heritage. Given the enormity of the task on a national scale, however, consideration might be given to adopting a more streamlined approach.

The end product for each team should consist specifically of three elements: a brief historical account, a comprehensive set of photogrammetry elevations and plan or a 3D digital model, and a photographic survey. Because there is only work for one or two people in each of these elements, the team should be small in number so that all involved can fully engage. The recruitment of team members should focus on individuals with the appropriate aptitudes, interest and equipment. While this was not a problem in Ballydehob, it might well be so in other communities. This issue might be addressed by recruiting a small number of suitable individuals from several neighbouring communities to work together in a single team and share their equipment, knowledge and time to document a number of harbours in their wider geographical area. It would also be helpful, where possible, to initially identify an individual in the locality who might be in a position to advise or take the lead in recruiting potentially suitable personnel. All of this, of course, would require promotion and coordination at a national level by a central administrative body or organisation and the introduction of a permanent digital archive.

If this approach smacks of exclusivity, it is due to necessity. While much can be said for the involvement of the wider community, as a means of promoting public awareness and appreciation of local heritage, the immediate priority of this particular proposal is the speedy, accurate, and comprehensive documentation of a significant and highly vulnerable section of that heritage.

The Team

Tom Vaughan – A professional drone pilot and aerial photographer. His clients include An Garda Síochána (the Irish police force), Netflix, and Sky TV.

Julianna O'Donoghue – Director of Mizen Archaeology, providing commercial underwater and land-based archaeological services. As well as archaeological surveying, monitoring, and excavation, her work includes the completion of the cultural heritage components of Environmental Impact Assessment Reports.

Kevin O'Farrell – A professional photographer of international standing, with a particular focus on maritime heritage. He has exhibited in Ireland, England, Germany and Poland.

Sara Canty – Journalist and community organiser who uses her skills to promote and support local interests.

Denis O'Brien – Quantity Surveyor with a rich family heritage in local building construction.

Finola Finlay and Robert Harris – Finola is a retired college dean and Robert is a retired architect. They run the Roaringwater Journal blog, publishing articles on a wide range of disciplines, including history, archaeology, and architecture.

Eoin Fannon – A practising barrister with a particular interest in maritime issues. He has also worked in physical oceanography and fisheries research. He is a regular contributor to conferences on the law of the sea and the marine environment.

Eugene McSweeney – A retired teacher, local historian and organiser of heritage events, lectures and walks.

Anke Eckardt – Wooden boat builder, artist, and model maker, with a BSc degree in experimental physics.

Brian Lalor – An artist and writer with a background in architecture and archaeology in the Middle East. He has been director of a number of Irish national arts organisations and founder/curator of a local arts museum and an art gallery.

Anne-Marie Birken – The current owner of the buildings on the quay, her expertise in the area of title deeds and conveyances proved very useful in tracing the occupancy history of the buildings.

John Forde – A retired businessman who is heavily involved in community projects. As Chairman of the Ballydehob Tidy Towns Committee, he actively promotes public interest in our built heritage as well as in wider environmental issues.

Cormac Levis – A retired teacher, maritime historian, and scion of a local family of boatmen, he has written extensively on local traditional workboats as well as contributed to television and radio documentaries on the subject.

References

Ballydehob Community. 1994. *History of Seafaring Community*. Interviews by Cormac Levis. Unpublished.

Courtenay, W. Chair. 1845. *Evidence taken before Her Majesty's Commissioners of Inquiry into the State of the Law and Practice in Respect to the Occupation of land in Ireland. Part II. [C 616] H.C. xx*. Dublin: Alexander Thom. https://parlipapers-proquest-com.ucd.idm.oclc.org/parlipapers/docview/t70.d75.1845-022467?accountid=14507

Hickey, Patrick. 2002. *Famine in West Cork, The Mizen Peninsula, Land and People 1800–1852*. Cork: Mercier Press.

Levis, Cormac. 1996. "The Almost Forgotten Harbour." *Mizen Journal No.4, Mizen Archaeological and Historical Society*: 105–126.

Levis, Cormac. 1997. "Sands of Time." *Mizen Journal No.5, Mizen Archaeological and Historical Society*: 108–130.

Levis, Cormac. 2008. "The Sandboats of Ballydehob." In *Traditional Boats of Ireland, History, Folklore and Construction*, edited by Críostóir Mac Cárthaigh, 285–295. Cork: The Collins Press.

McAfee, Patrick. 2009. *Lime Works, Using Lime in Traditional and New Buildings*. Dublin: The Building Limes Forum of Ireland.

O'Malley, Patricia. 1999. "Missing Friends From Schull Parish." *Mizen Journal No.7, Mizen Archaeological and Historical Society*: 20–28.

Epilogue

8 The Future of Harbour Heritage

Linde Egberts and Elizabeth Shotton

Introduction

As discussed in the preceding chapters, the rapidly increasing impact of climate change on coastal communities and their heritage has highlighted the largely undocumented status of small coastal piers and quays (Chapter 2). Part of the solution could lie in using inexpensive digital survey technologies, not only by national agencies and researchers (Chapters 4 and 6) but also by communities, allowing them to play a role in creating permanent records for these structures (Chapters 5, 6, and 7). Equally important is the reconsideration of heritage classification and analysis methodologies to properly capture the salient aspects of this heritage (Chapter 3) and a possible expansion to the range of actors involved in the documentation effort to include the engineers primarily responsible for these structures (Chapter 2).

There remain other questions concerning appropriate climate adaption strategies for such structures that are, as yet, largely unaddressed among the international community. With such a large inventory of coastal heritage under threat globally, difficult choices may be required as to how much should be saved and at what cost. The conversation which follows between Elizabeth Shotton, a specialist in digital documentation of harbours in Ireland, and Dr Linda Egberts, a specialist in critical approaches to landscape, spatial planning, climate change, and resilience, reflects on the future of coastal heritage within this context to expand the discussion from previous chapters. The conversation reviews ideas of peripherality, or what it means for heritage to be marginalised by traditional heritage canons; the complex risk posed to coastal heritage by the impacts of climate change; and the role that communities might play in defining the future of their heritage with the agencies responsible for its oversight, all of which is underpinned by the questions surrounding future adaptation strategies.

This chapter is an edited and rewritten version of the dialogue held in December 2022.[1]

Peripherality

Shotton: One of the interesting things you have discussed in your work is that there's a problematic differentiation between landscape and cultural heritage. Can you elaborate on that?

Egberts: In the heritage studies field, there has been a lot of emphasis on expert knowledge over knowledge by local communities or indigenous knowledge. It's protection-oriented and focused on monuments as individual objects rather than about landscapes as a whole, and traditionally relatively Eurocentric.

Thankfully, in the course of the last three decades there has been a paradigm shift that brings heritage and landscape studies quite close together. Landscapes and heritage have become perceived more as the process of interaction of humans with their environments, which are in a constant state of change. Attention has also shifted towards power relationships that shape heritage and landscape values, including indigenous and local non-expert knowledge in these fields.

Shotton: That seems to be key here – that heritage goals have to align with other goals to create a negotiated solution. You have used the term *peripheral heritage* in reference to coastal heritage – can you explain that term?

Egberts: I meant peripheral not only in the geographical sense. At that time, I was working with coastal regions in Europe, far away from urban centres. They shared the characteristic that they were mostly left out of the national heritage canons. An example would be the Norwegian outports (Figure 1.1), which are villages, built almost entirely out of wooden houses, along the coast and the rocky shores on the fjords. These were seafaring communities, but they weren't a part of what became regarded as the quintessential Norwegian landscape Egberts, Linde, and Dag Hundstad. 2019. The national trend to articulate its distinctiveness from Denmark and other nations meant that other landscapes and heritage were nationally appropriated: fjords, mountains, glaciers, and folk traditions from scarcely populated, isolated inlands. The South Norwegian outports were too European, and too intercultural to fit this purpose. This meant that the wooden houses had a lower priority in the heritage preservation scheme (Egberts and Hundstad 2019).

Shotton: This brings to mind recent efforts to document important coastal heritage in Wales and Ireland. There are things that are considered quintessentially Irish like old ring mounds and forts that are thousands of years old, or natural heritage features such as cliffs. Whereas small piers and quays, though quintessential to many

Figure 8.1 The outport Ny-Hellesund in Agder, South Norway photographed by Linde Egberts 2016.

Irish communities until the mid-20th century, do not figure significantly in the national mindset of what counts as heritage.

Egberts: Maybe you know the book, *Imagined Communities*, by Benedict Anderson (2006), who writes about four types of symbols that a nation needs. The uses of the past play a role in each of the four types of symbols, but only when it can serve a particular purpose; the ways heritage is selected play a part in the construction of identity as described by Anderson. In my research, I argued that heritage is only appropriated when it can live up to a certain narrative role in present-day society. It can be the foundational story – where do we come from? What is the origin of our nation, of our region? The other one is the Golden Age – the age in which a particular region was wealthier, and more successful than its neighbours, the heyday of cultural wealth, of power. The third one that heritage gets assigned is the role of a recent collective trauma (Egberts and Hundstad 2019). For example, in Zeeland in the Netherlands, the big flood of 1953 was a significant regional identity denominator since the 1950s for communities that had suffered massively. If heritage cannot live up to one of these roles, the likelihood that it gets used in heritage policy, preservation measures, or tourism campaigns is small. Heritage experts play a pivotal role in the selection, preservation and representation of heritage, be it national,

	regional or local. Heritage scholars call these dominant narratives *authorised*.
Shotton:	What do we do about the heritage that is peripheral to those narratives?
Egberts:	That depends on what communities want of course. If they're seeking recognition, they need to contest the *authorized heritage narrative*, which is what critical heritage studies are all about. In many cases, I think the question of *why* societies preserve certain heritage objects, buildings or landscapes has not really been answered. How can people then be sure they still want to pursue this preservation for the future? I think heritage experts and communities need to ask ourselves more of these future-oriented questions. Like: 'For whom do we preserve? For what type of future? What will this place look like and how should this heritage be preserved?' If they begin to question why they need this heritage, they might conclude they do not want to preserve everything that is now listed. And that opens up room for new engagements with heritage, such as *adaptive release* or ruination (DeSilvey et al. 2021). Engaging actively with heritage can also mean that we consciously disengage and create room for new values and future trajectories.

Climate Change

Shotton:	Could I ask you about your current interest in critical heritage approaches and their relationship to climate change?
Egberts:	The climate crisis really crept into my work when I was studying the influence of tourism on urban and rural landscapes, particularly in coastal landscapes. Researchers and policymakers cannot work with heritage landscapes without taking climate challenges into account. It's time to see how heritage knowledge can lead to better decision-making about landscapes under climate change.
Shotton:	You have suggested that the heritage sector could learn from climate science.
Egberts:	Climate scientists try to get as concrete an image of the future as they can, by the means that they have available. Heritage professionals have for a very long time been preserving things for future generations without really making explicit what the future looks like. They have often approached heritage as a set of historic objects that need to be maintained for a future that is a seemingly stable continuation of the present (Harvey and Perry 2015). Climate scientists more often look at landscapes as a set of processes that are in a constant state of change. I think this process-based approach, in which understanding the future as different from the present, is important for heritage too.

Shotton: Are you suggesting that they have to reimagine how society might change as well as acknowledging that these things that are conserved, whether they're landscapes, objects, or buildings, are in a constant state of change?

Egberts: Yes. The harbours discussed in this book are, of course, dramatic and fantastic examples of places where things are inevitably changing and not everything that communities value as heritage can be preserved indefinitely. I'm not an expert in the coastal landscapes that you study. But I do know that climate change is felt in different ways in different places and the harbour locations are very often at the forefront of vulnerability. The question I am interested in is if this material heritage can no longer be preserved, how can communities use their heritage in different ways to deal with the changes they are confronted with?

Climate Imaginaries

Shotton: In thinking about collective constructions of the idea of heritage, particularly in the face of climate change, in one of your recent articles, *Plans for Uncertain Futures* (Riesto et al. 2022), you use the term *climate imaginaries* regarding coastal climate adaptation. What do you mean by climate imaginaries?

Egberts: Climate imaginaries are the ways in which societies or actors in societies shape an image in their minds about what climate and climate change are. These include depictions, affect, and ways of apprehending the climate's past. This includes ideas about whether climates were stable in the past and how culture and nature are related.

These climate imaginaries are intertwined with heritage. Pictorial traditions are used to communicate climate urgency. Think of a flooded Venice in which carnival-goers walk over elevated wooden platforms to keep their feet dry. Or the polar bear on a melting flow of ice. Those images are rooted in long pictorial traditions that go well beyond the climate crisis or photography. So even if we're not talking about heritage being threatened by climate change, there is a relationship between cultural traditions, ways of seeing and valuing, that makes the relationship between heritage and climate change multi-directional and complex.

Shotton: Meaning the imaginaries that we hold or are drawn to impact how we think about coastal climate adaptation, but equally the adaptation can influence the imaginaries?

Egberts: There's a back-and-forth between these things. Both climate adaptation planning and heritage preservation are future-making processes, as David Harvey and John Perry (2015) call them: people

	project their current values, which are rooted in the past, onto the future.
Shotton:	What does that mean for coastal heritage and climate adaptation? Can we make use of imaginaries to draw out or give shape to a better future?
Egberts:	I think so. If heritage experts, local communities, planning professionals, and politicians, are more aware of these parallels, it would be easier to get into a conversation with each other. That can enable cooperation and create new qualities by doing so. Together, these stakeholders can approach heritage and climate adaptation as a joint effort.
Shotton:	Caitlin DeSilvey's work seems to draw in some of the ways of thinking about narratives and how we consider heritage going forward and potential loss. Do you want to say something about her work?
Egberts:	I think she's one of the key people who currently breaks open the heritage paradigm without abandoning it. Over the past century or so, heritage experts have successfully promoted and maintained the material aspects of heritage, for instance by restoring historic buildings. Contrary to general assumptions, heritage approaches have a lot to offer, even when traditional preservation strategies are no longer feasible. DeSilvey (2017) argues that different kinds of interaction are possible with heritage materiality, each other, and with the non-human world once we let go of this traditional preservation response.
Shotton:	How does that affect a community that might be in jeopardy of losing the heritage that they value, like small coastal communities? And I'm thinking of some of the harbour communities that I have worked with, like Ballydehob in County Cork, where many of the quays are falling into disrepair. The memory of being such an active maritime settlement is disappearing before the communities' eyes. How do they cope with the impending loss?
Egberts:	Acknowledging that this is a very impactful thing is really important. I think what we can learn from DeSilvey is that we have to accept the fact that some things are beyond saving. If we change our focus towards acknowledging the mourning process, new interactions with the memories can also emerge. If we stop being defensive about material loss, we might discover that materiality is not the only *aide-memoire*. We can also create new aids of memory.
Shotton:	But how does the community then hold on to that memory of what they had been as a community if they let go of the material as an aid of memory? What are the processes or avenues to do that?

Egberts: There are many different options, of course. A Danish example is Rubjerg Knude lighthouse, in an area threatened by coastal erosion. Technicians put it on rails and made a big ceremony out of moving it away from the sea by 70 meters. Along with lots more losses in the area, the 'authentic' location of the lighthouse was given up. Nevertheless, its ceremonial move had a function.

In contrast, DeSilvey writes about a community in Cornwall that actually did not want a memorial for the harbour that they had lost, they wanted to experience the obsolescence rather than having an artefact that would anchor the memory in place.

Shotton: The story about that Cornwall harbour where they're planning to let it go to ruin, which is part of the discussion on managed retreats in the UK, is emblematic. One of the reasons I'm interested in documenting these structures is so that we have a record of them before this happens. But the problem with letting a harbour fall to ruin is that they become hazards for boating. And it raises the whole issue of whether you let a thing fall apart and become a hazard, or do you actually take it down.

Egberts: The process of documenting something before it disappears is in a way scientific, but it can also be quite therapeutic. It can be a way to help academics and communities accept the fact that something is gone, and if they can't hold on to the materiality, they can at least hold on to its recorded memory in some sort of database.

Letting things become a hazard is also part of coastal history. Boats that have sunk have always been hazards to other boats that have to tread the same waters. Regardless, there can be value creation in doing the latter – in embracing and documenting the demolition of heritage purposefully and meaningfully. This process can also create community, new memories and even new heritage values.

Shotton: Unfortunately, the local councils are probably never going to find the money to carefully take something apart. So, they may just let it fall apart.

Egberts: They probably need a contingency plan for potential accidents, so they could also consider it an investment. But then it is about coastal safety: funds for rescuing and emergencies come from a different budget than heritage conservation. When people can find each other – in local communities, on a regional level, maybe even on a national level, and align their agendas, one investment can serve multiple purposes. I think these intersectoral conversations are very important to enable heritage practices to serve larger societal purposes like climate resilience.

Community

Shotton: There are a lot of cross- or interdisciplinary conversations that have to start to happen around these maritime structures. At the local level, the engineers are tasked with taking care of the harbours and heritage officers are tasked with deciding whether it's heritage. And, as you suggest, there is probably input needed from the Coast Guard.

Egberts: Thinking out-of-the-box with alliances can be relevant, in this case, insurance companies for instance. In that sense, the climate emergency is no different from other planning assignments. The sense of urgency however is often quite high in climate dialogues, which might sometimes make it harder to get people around the table. Studies in the Netherlands and Denmark indicate that policymakers and planners tend to focus more on their own sectoral approaches (Fatorić and Egberts 2020).

Shotton: And yet there is a sense of emergency about climate change. How do we avoid that retreat into our own disciplines because we're feeling threatened by something imminent?

Egberts: It's a very difficult one. If you are already in that state of emergency, I think realizing that you are and saying, OK, it's going happen anyway, we might as well take a step back, take a few weeks extra, have a few extra cups of coffee with people that we would normally not speak to – that can make such a difference.

Shotton: So, there needs to be some kind of negotiation on the part of national policy, regional obligations, and the communities about what to save and maintain, and whether some can be lost.

Egberts: This means the transition from one heritage paradigm to another. Heritage experts might have to shift into a different gear in order to spend public money in a responsible way: away from preservation and towards approaches like adaptive release. It's an ethical question as well because the municipalities who spend money on endangered heritage, are sometimes also the ones having a hard time keeping the schools open, or other challenges to maintain quality of life within the community. How do we keep this municipality, and this community alive and also take care of our heritage?

Shotton: Does that conversation happen on a national policy-based platform and drip feed down to the regional governments that have to handle this situation? Or are there other avenues to shifting this current paradigm and the legislation surrounding it?

Egberts: Sometimes local communities can be frontrunners in saying that we have to let go of this paradigm because it goes to the cost of our livelihood or quality of life. But in many other cases renewal in the heritage sector is slow and comes, at least for the Netherlands, through interdisciplinary national funding programs. We have seen quite a few of them since the Internationale Bauausstellung Emscher Park (1989–1999) in Germany accelerated the experimentation with adaptive reuse of post-industrial wastelands. In the Netherlands we have seen a similar project called Belvedere (1999–2009) and more recently the Heritage Deal (*Erfgoed Deal*), which offers matching funds for interdisciplinary, intersectoral and participatory projects on heritage, landscape, ecology and sustainability. By funding example projects and learning from them, the hope is that the lessons learnt will influence policy.

Shotton: Are there specific case studies you could point to that are exemplars of that process?

Egberts: One project I love in the Netherlands is the water mill landscape in the Dommel River in the south of the Netherlands (Erfgoed Deal n.d.). There were quite a few traditional water mills left, but their historic water retention capacity was lost. By rewetting the river landscape in multiple places, the area is now able to buffer more water in wet months, preventing flooding in the downstream city of Den Bosch. In dry periods, the retained water prevents drought in the larger area. As the Dommel flows through urbanised areas, its wetter landscape also buffers heat stress more effectively. The focus shifted from monument preservation to learning from historic landscape practices to regain its resilience in changing conditions.

Shotton: Are those conversations limited to experts or can the community have a role in that discussion?

Egberts: The community can have an important role. In some cases, the heritage interpretations by experts are contested by citizens, who feel that their heritage values are not recognised enough in the existing heritage canons. Think of the demonstrations surrounding colonial memorial statues in public spaces in many parts of the Western world. In some cases, heritage experts value older objects more than more recent ones, which can be linked to the memories of local families. Citizens therefore have different time horizons than experts and can challenge expert interpretations. I see it as a necessity that we have dialogues about whose heritage we preserve. It's about who *owns* the past, but also about who *owns* the future.

Shotton: How do we enable communities to have these conversations with the people who are charged with making these decisions?

Egberts: By taking the 2005 Faro Convention as a source of inspiration. The convention says that heritage can be a means to create more diverse and inclusive societies. It needs to be a possibility for all people in society and that also forces experts to rethink their position from being the person who makes the final decision on what to keep and what not to list to becoming a moderator of a conversation. And being a much better listener than a decision-maker or sender of information. Good examples like the harbour heritage project can help heritage experts rethink and reinvent their own role in society.

Note

1 Recordings and transcripts are stored by Elizabeth Shotton.

References

Anderson, Benedict. 2006. *Imagined Communities: Reflections on the Origin and Spread of Nationalism*. London, New York: Verso.

DeSilvey, Caitlin. 2017. *Curated Decay: Heritage Beyond Saving*. Minneapolis: University of Minnesota Press.

DeSilvey, Caitlin, et al. 2021. "When Loss Is More: From Managed Decline to Adaptive Release." *The Historic Environment: Policy & Practice* 12 (3): 418–433. https://doi.org/10.1080/17567505.2021.1957263

Egberts, Linde, and Dag Hundstad. 2019. "Coastal Heritage in Touristic Regional Identity Narratives: A Comparison between the Norwegian Region Sørlandet and the Dutch Wadden Sea Area." *International Journal of Heritage Studies* 25 (10): 1073–1087. https://doi.org/10.1080/13527258.2019.1570310

Erfgoed Deal. n.d. "Watermolenlandschappen." *Projecten: Water en bodem*. Accessed 28 March, 2023. www.erfgoeddeal.nl/projecten/water-en-bodem/watermolenlandschappen-voor-klimaatadaptatie

Fatorić, Sandra, and Linde Egberts. 2020. "Realising the Potential of Cultural Heritage to Achieve Climate Change Actions in the Netherlands." *Journal of Environmental Management* 274: 111107. https://doi.org/10.1016/j.jenvman.2020.111107

Harvey, D., and J. Perry, eds. 2015. *The Future of Heritage as Climates Change: Loss, Adaptation and Creativity*. London: Routledge.

Riesto, Svava et al. 2022. "Plans for Uncertain Futures: Heritage and Climate Imaginaries in Coastal Climate Adaptation." *International Journal of Heritage Studies* 28: 358–375.

Resources for Communities

Databases & Websites

Archwilio. 2023. https://archwilio.org.uk/wp/
Cadw. 2023. https://cadw.gov.wales/advice-support/cof-cymru/search-cadw-records
Coflein. 2023. https://coflein.gov.uk/en/
Galway County Council. 2016. "Piers and Harbours of Galway County." *Galway Open Data Portal*. https://opendata-galwaycoco.hub.arcgis.com/datasets/galwaycoco::piers-and-harbours-of-galway-county/about
Harbourview. 2023. www.historicharboursofirelandandwales.com/
Minor Harbours of Ireland (MHI). 2019. https://digital.ucd.ie/view/ucdlib:255666
National Monuments Service. 2023a. *Historic Environment Viewer*. Ireland. https://maps.archaeology.ie/HistoricEnvironment/
National Monuments Service. 2023b. "National Monuments Service – Archaeological Survey of Ireland Dataset." *Local Government Department of Housing, and Heritage* (Online: Data.gov.ie). https://data.gov.ie/dataset/national-monuments-service-archaeological-survey-of-ireland?package_type=dataset
NIAH. 2023a. "National Inventory of Architectural Heritage (NIAH) National Dataset." *Local Government Department of Housing, and Heritage* (Online: Data.Gov.ie). https://data.gov.ie/dataset/national-inventory-of-architectural-heritage-niah-national-dataset?package_type=dataset
The SCAPE Trust. 2023. https://scapetrust.org/
Underwater Archaeology Unit. 2002. *Piers, Ports and Harbours: Draft Inventory in 2 Volumes*. Dublin: National Monument Service of Ireland (Unpublished. Available to view on request).

Guidance Documents

A Practical Guide to Recording Archaeological Sites. 2011. Allander: Royal Commission on the Ancient and Historical Monuments of Scotland (RCAHMS). https://webarchive.nrscotland.gov.uk/3/https://scotlandsruralpast.org.uk/images/pdfs/SRP%20Manual%20single%20page.pdf
Barker, L., and A. Corns, eds. 2023. *CHERISH: Sharing Our Practice. Investigating Heritage and Climate Change in Coastal and Maritime Environments. A Guide to the CHERISH Toolkit*. Aberystwyth: CHERISH/RCAHMW. https://cherishproject.eu/en/resources/reports/sharing-our-practice/

FISH – Forum on Information Standards in Heritage. 2015. *Historic Characterisation Thesaurus*. Accessed 24 February, 2023. www.heritage-standards.org.uk/
Hamond, Fred, and Mary McMahon. 2002. *Recording and Conserving Ireland's Industrial Heritage: An Introductory Guide*. Kilkenny: The Heritage Council. www.heritagecouncil.ie/content/files/recording_conserving_irelands_industrial_heritage_guide_2002_8mb.pdf
Heritage Council (Ireland). 2006. *Conserving Ireland's Maritime Heritage*. Kilkenny: The Heritage Council. www.heritagecouncil.ie/content/files/conserving_irelands_maritime_heritage_2006_2mb.pdf
Heritage Council (Ireland)/ 2017. *Guidance for Community Archaeology Projects*. Kilkenny: The Heritage Council. www.heritagecouncil.ie/content/files/Guidance_for_community_archaeology_projects.pdf
NIAH. 2023b. *National Inventory of Architectural Heritage Handbook*. Dublin: National Inventory of Architectural Heritage (NIAH). www.buildingsofireland.ie/app/uploads/2023/04/NIAH-Handbook-Edition-April-2023.pdf

Index

Note: Page numbers in *italics* indicate a figure and page numbers in **bold** indicate a table on the corresponding page.

Aasleigh Pier, County Galway *22*, 23
Aberaeron, Wales 44, 46
Abercastle, Wales 44, *45*
actors 93, 97
adaptive release 96, 100
airborne LiDAR Bathymetry 72
anchorage, anchorages 3, 42, 44, 46, 51
AR (Augmented reality) 73
Archaeological Services 15–16
archive, archives 25, 64, 67, 46
audits 16, 19–20, 21, 22, 23–24

Ballydehob, County Cork *6*, 7, 9, 20; aerial view of *79*; geographical and historical context 78–82; small satellite quays *6*, 20, 82–86
Bathymetry 70–72
beaches 24, 42
Birken, Anne-Marie 87
Breakwater, breakwaters 30, 31, 33, 36, 44, 50
British Fisheries Society (BFS) 29–30
Brough Pier, Scotland 36
Bullock/Bulloch Harbour, Ireland 4, *4*, 5, 57

Cadw 47, 49
Canmore: database 8; record 33
Canty, S. 82
Carmarthen, Wales 46
catch-pier 31
CITiZAN project 6, 7, 49, 51
Clare Coastal Survey of 2008 22, *23*
classification, in heritage management 28–29

climate: adaptation 5, 7, 9, 10, 93, 97, 98; change 3–6, 8, 72, 96–97; crisis 96, 97; dialogues 100; emergency 49, 51, 100; imaginaries 97–102; impact 3–6; urgency 97
Climate, Heritage and Environments of Reefs, Islands and Headlands (CHERISH) 5, 6, 7, 49–51
cloud storage 65
coastal communities 56, 93, 98
coastal erosion 8, 99
coastal safety 5, 99
Coastie initiative 8
CoastSnap 8
Coliemore, Ireland 57
communication 9, 51
community/communities 1; engagement 7, 10, 23–24, 58; local 8–9; participation 6–9
Cornwall 32, 69, 99
cove 44; Barley Cove, County Cork 81; Mullion Cove, Cornwall 69
cultural landscape 56, 65–66

Dalkey Island, Ireland 57
damage 5, 6, 21, 23, 50
deterioration 15, 21
Dewisland, Wales 44, *45*
digital: access to records 65–66; archive 87; model, models, modelling 2, 61, 70, 72–73, 86, 87; photogrammetry 50, 55, 70, 84, 87; photographs 65; photography 64; recording 7, 67, 72, 82; records 64–65; technologies 70, 93

Index

digital tools: mapping and engagement 73–74; morphology 72
documentation 1, 6, 7, 8–9, 20, 82, 93; advanced methods of 59; approaches and inputs 86–87; non-destructive 70; traditional methods 59
drone, drones 49, 62, 70
Dublin Bay, Ireland 4–5

Easterling, K. 69
Eckardt, A. 82, 86
engagement 23–24, 73–74
engineers 3, 5, 16, 25, 31–32, 93, 100
entering vestibule 31
estuary 42

Faro Convention on the Value of Cultural Heritage for Society 6
Finlay, F. 86
Fishguard 42, 47, *48*, 49
forecasting 72
Forum on Information Standards in Heritage (FISH) 29
framework 15–16, 32, 36–38, *38*
freehand sketches 58, *58*
Freswick Pier, Caithness 36, *37*
future planning 7

Gaeltacht 19, *19*
Gleesk harbour, County Kerry 7, *8*
Graham, A 2, 28, 30, 33
Granada Convention 16
Greenmount Quay, County Cork 86, *86*
groyne wall 30, 39n3; *see also* breakwater

hand-held photographs 59
harbours/harbour-works 2, 3, 7, 16, 28, 29, 30, 31, 39, 56, 57, 66, 69; Bullock Harbour (Ireland) 4, *4*; Gleesk harbour, County Kerry 7, *8*; historic harbours of Wales 43–46; minor 3, 29, 32, 39; pan-Wales distribution map *43*, **44**; records (*see* records); small-scale 28–38; Scottish 2, 28
Harbourview project 7, 67, 73 *68*, *71*, *73*, 82
Harris, R. 86
heritage: approaches 98; authorized 96; coastal 1, 2–3, 4, 10, 49, 67, 69, 93, 98; conservation 99; critical 96; experts 95, 96, 98, 100, 101, 102; industrial 3, 16, 18; intangible 67, 70; interpretations 101; marginal 68–69; maritime 2–3, 82; narrative 96; paradigm 98, 100; peripheral 94; preservation 9, 94, 96, 97, 98, 100; recording 15–16, 22, 32, 67–74; sector 5, 96, 101; stakeholders 67, *68*; values 99, 101
heritage engineering works (HEW) 16
Historic Environment (Wales) Act 2016 47
Historic Environment Records (HERs) 47, 49
historic harbours: recording 55–66; of Wales 43–46
Historic Seascape Characterisation (HSC) 29
Hume, J. 28

inclined plane 32, 36
industrial: archeologist 28; -era dock 42; harbours 32; heritage 3, 16–18, *17*, 74; inertia 69; sites 16
infrastructure 2, 18, 31, 42, 44, 46, 49, 74, 82
inlets 42, 44
inter-tidal 49, 50, 51
inventory/inventories 15–16; and community engagement 23–24; of landing places 16–22, **18**; of piers 16–22, **18**; of quays 16–22, **18**; topics found in 21; types, levels of 22
Ireland 2, 3–4, 8, 15–16, 19, 20, 25, 67; Bullock Harbour 4, *4*; historic harbours 64; Ordnance Survey in 15

Jackson, G. 2, 28
Jenkins, J. G. 43
Jervis, A. 2
jette/jetty/gette 30

Kilkee Pier, County Clare *23*

Lalor, B. 86
landing places 3, 28, 29, 32, 42, 44, 46; inventories of 16–22, 24 **18**
landing slip 37
landscape 65–66, 94

laser scanning 59, 62, 72
LiDAR/Lidar 15, 72
local communities 8–9, 10, 24, 87, 100

maintenance 3, 5, 18, 25, 82
mapping 6, 7, 73–74
marginal heritage 68–69
marginality 38
maritime cultural landscape 2
materiality 30, 33, 36, 39, 98, 99
McKeague, P. 8, 24
monitoring 8, 47, 50–51
morphology 72
Morris, L. 49

National Inventory of Architectural Heritage (NIAH) 16, 18, 28; guidelines 23
National Monument Act 15
National Monuments Record of Wales (NMRW) 44, 46–47
National Monuments Service 20
National Primary Record Number (NPRN) 44, *48*
National Trust (NT) 47
Newport Parrog, Wales 6, *68*
non-destructive documentation 70

O'Brien, D. 87
O'Donoghue, J. 82, 86
Office of Public Works (OPW) 20, 22
on-site drawings 15
Ordnance Survey, in Ireland 15
orthomosaic 47, *48*
overtopping 4, *4*, 5, 33, 36

participation 6–9
participatory governance 10; models/management 7; planning 70; projects 101
peripherality 94–96
photogrammetry *48*, *68*, 50, *50*, 70, 84
photography 59, *60*; digital 65; off-site, level of skill required 62, 64; off-site processing 59, 61–62; on-site, level of skill required 62
photomodels/photomodelling 61, *61*, 62
photomosaics 55, *56*, 59, 62, *63*
physical access to records 65–66
physical records 64–65
pier/piers/peer 66; inventories of 16–22, **18**; Rockfield 32–36, *33*, *34–35*
pinnings 84–85

point cloud 62, 64
Porthclais, Wales 44, *45*, 47, 50, *50*
Porth Dinllaen, Wales 44
Porthgain, Wales 44, *45*
Porthmadog, Wales 46
ports 1, 2, 16, 28, 31, 32, 72; hierarchy 31
Primary Record Number (PRN) 47
protective slope 33, *35*
public engagement 50

quay/quays/key: Ballydehob 78–82; inventories of 16–22, **18**; small satellite 20, 82–86

Recording and Conserving Ireland's Industrial Heritage: An Introductory Guide 16, *17*
Record of Protected Status (RPS) 16, 18
records 18, 21, 25, 28, 29, 37, 42, 46, 47, 49–51, 93; creation in advance of destruction 15, 72; digital 64–65; digital access to 65–66; Historic Context 56–57; Office of Public Works 20; physical 64–65; physical access to 65–66; purpose of making 55; survey methods and 57–66
rectified photography 59, 82
regional 7, 8, 9, 15, 20, 25, 38, 42, 46–47, 51, 95, 96, 100
remote sensing 55, 72
resilience 5, 99, 101
risk 3, 5, 6, 9, 15, 30, 69, 72, 93
risk register 15
river 37, 44, 46, 101
robots 72
Rockfield, Scotland 32–36, *33*, *34–35*, 37–38, *38*
Royal Commission on the Ancient and Historical Monuments of Wales (RCAHMW) 28, 46, 47, 50, 51

Sandycove, Ireland 4, *56*
scaling, photograph 59
Scotland 2, 3, 6
Scottish Archaeological Research Framework (ScARF) 16, 17–18
sea level rise 1, 5, 50
significance 18, 21, 23, 28, 32, 39, 74
Sites and Monuments Record (SMR) 16, 18
sketching 57–58, *58*

small satellite quays, Ballydehob 20, 82–86
small-scale harbours 28–38; see also harbours
Smeaton, J. 31
Solva, Wales 44, *45*
Stevenson, T. 30
storms 1, 5, 69
structures 5–6, 36

talus wall 33, *35*
taxonomy 28–29, 30–31, 32, 38
template *17*, 20
The Planning and Development Act, 2000 64
Thomas, D. 8, 24
threat 1, 4, 10, 18, 57, 93

tide 3, 4–5, 35, 36, 44, 74
topography 70–72
traditional methods, documentation 59
two converging piers 30

Underwater Archaeology Unit (UAU) 20

valorisation 67, 74
Vaughan, T. 82

Wales 67; historic harbours of 43–46; role of national and regional organisations within 46–47
Westerdahl, C. 2
Wharf 32
Wilkhaven Pier, Scotland 36

For Product Safety Concerns and Information please contact our EU representative GPSR@taylorandfrancis.com
Taylor & Francis Verlag GmbH, Kaufingerstraße 24, 80331 München, Germany

www.ingramcontent.com/pod-product-compliance
Lightning Source LLC
Chambersburg PA
CBHW051755230426
43670CB00012B/2301